Nicolson *on* Sails

Cruising and Racing Sail Tips

Ian Nicolson

ADLARD COLES NAUTICAL
London

Dedication

To Tim, Beth (Liz), Philippa and Alexander Jalland.

Also to Dick Hughes who started our company, Nicolson Hughes Sails, with me, and to the people who have put in many hours on the sail loft floor, often working overtime when things were hectic. The present team includes Cathy McAuley, Liz Montgomery, Maria Sharp and Christine Young (in alphabetical order, because some have worked so long with us that I am not sure who started first); also, to all the other lasses and lads who have helped make our sail loft a cheerful, successful organisation.

This book is for boat owners and crews, as well as amateur and professional sailmakers. A selection of these drawings first appeared in the magazine *Yachting Life*, and my thanks go to the founder and editor, Alistair Vallance.

Published 1998 by Adlard Coles Nautical
an imprint of A & C Black (Publishers) Ltd
35 Bedford Row, London WC1R 4JH

Copyright © Ian Nicolson 1998

ISBN 0–7136–4468–0

A CIP catalogue record for this book is available from the British Library.

Typeset in 10 on 12pt Concorde
Printed and bound in Great Britain by Butler and Tanner Ltd, Frome and London

Other books by Ian Nicolson

Build Your Own Boat
Improve Your Own Boat
Boat Data Book
Cold Moulded and Strip Plank Wood Boatbuilding
Build a Simply Dinghy (with Alasdair Reynolds)
Race Winner (with Richard Nicolson)
The Log of the Maken
Sea Saint
Building the St Mary
Small Steel Craft
Surveying Small Craft
Designer's Notebook
Marinise Your Boat
A Guide to Boat Buying
Yacht Designers Sketchbook
Comfort in the Cruising Yacht
Roving in Open Boats
The Ian Nicolson Omnibus
Outboard Boats and Engines
Dinghy Cruising

Contents

1. Mainsails

A modern mainsail

All sorts of yachts are changing to fully battened mainsails with lazyjacks to get the advantages of easier handling, better performance upwind and down, and hopefully less wear. Existing mainsails can be converted, but unless the sail is in excellent condition it may well be cheaper in the long run to have a new sail specially made.

Converting an existing sail does not give the advantage of a big high roach which is so effective at improving windward and leeward speed. The battens can be homemade of wood to save money, but they are liable to break in wild weather. Glassfibre battens stand up to severe conditions, but they still fracture if over-bent, so a few spares should be carried.

When ordering a new sail of this sort it is important to realise that it should last longer than a traditional sail because it does not flog. The long battens keep the sail quiet and relatively docile. As the sail should last longer, it does not pay to cut down on the size or cost of any component.

Where the lazyjacks touch the batten pockets, chafe is common, but this is dealt with in Chapter 9 in the section on Bagnall-Wild

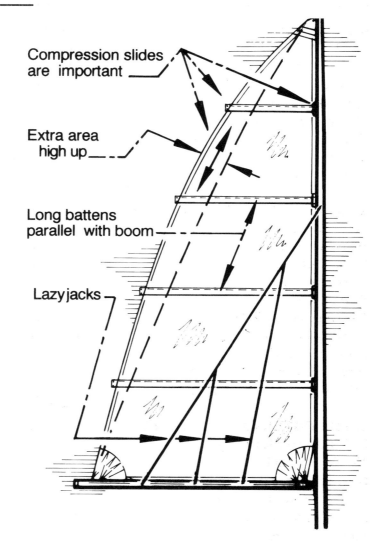

Compression slides are important

Extra area high up

Long battens parallel with boom

Lazyjacks

lazyjacks. The luff slides have to be specially made and at least slightly oversize. They also need to be inspected every week and must be kept clean. Some need regular lubrication. Above all, this is not a place for saving pennies.

The battens are set parallel to the boom to suit the reefs. However, if the boom tends to drag in the sea when reefed, it may pay to tilt the battens and reefs up at the aft end.

Mainsail foot measurements

The foot of a mainsail is measured from the back of the mast to the clew out-haul. The dimension is taken to the aft side of the hole through the clew eye, which is the same point as the aft face of the clew shackle pin.

Mainsails have to be hauled out tight along the boom, so there must be a short length of boom aft of the clew for the outhaul flexible wire, rope or lashing. Just how far the boom should extend is sometimes the subject of argument but as a rough guide there should be 1 in (about 25 mm) for every 6 ft (roughly 2 m) of the boat's overall length. Slightly too much boom length is much better than too little; with the latter, it can be hard or impossible to get the mainsail properly tensioned along the foot.

At the fore end of the boom, the foot of the mainsail cannot extend right to the mast but must be cut back so that the tack eye can be shackled or lashed to the eye on the boom aft of the gooseneck. When ordering a new mainsail, the sailmaker needs to be given the length of this cutback, or 'knock' or 'knock-back' as it is sometimes called.

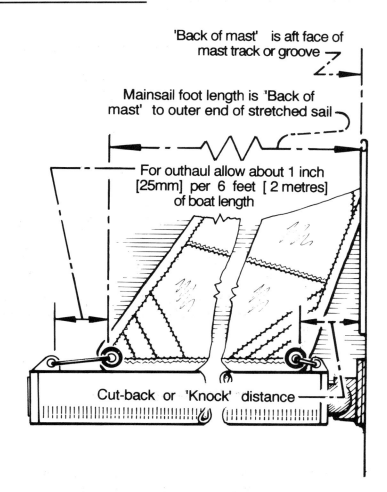

'Back of mast' is aft face of mast track or groove

Mainsail foot length is 'Back of mast' to outer end of stretched sail

For outhaul allow about 1 inch [25mm] per 6 feet [2 metres] of boat length

Cut-back or 'Knock' distance

Too much of a cut-back allows the wind to escape from the high pressure side of the sail to the leeward low pressure side, and this is certainly not something a racing owner can tolerate. Too small a 'knock' on the sail, and the tack will be baggy and ill-fitting, so that it may be necessary to take a lashing from the tack eye forward round the gooseneck, where it may suffer from chafe as the boom moves.

Mainsail foot slides

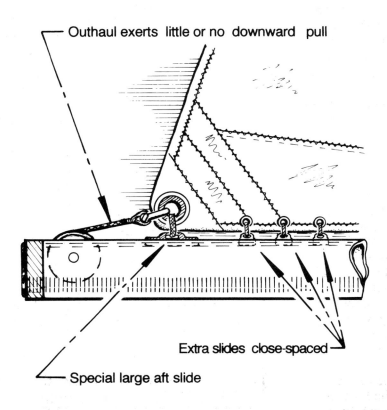

Outhaul exerts little or no downward pull

Special large aft slide

Extra slides close-spaced

The tension on the leech of a mainsail becomes very high in heavy winds. The upward pull is largely concentrated at the clew eye, and as a result breakages and other problems are common here. If the foot of the sail is roped, and the rope is in a groove or channel in the top of the boom, it is common for the foot rope to pull right out of the groove.

To defeat this tendency, careful sailmakers fit an extra-large metal slide to the clew eye. The bottom of the slide is typically five times as long as an ordinary slide, and has the same section as the foot rope. It is held by a strong tape, doubled round and well stitched to deal with the severe tension.

When there are slides along the foot of the sail, as shown here, it is advisable to have extra ones, close-spaced at the aft end, to help deal with this acute vertical pull. Sometimes these slides are of metal for extra strength and reliability, even though the rest of the slides are plastic.

Assessing mast bend

There are few things more difficult to measure than mast bend. Some people take photos of the yacht under way, then have large prints made and use these to measure the bend using the length of the yacht to establish the scale. (The height of the mast cannot be used, as the yacht will be at least slightly heeled, so the mast appears to be shorter than it is.) To get accuracy, the photos must be taken from the wind-ward and leeward sides, dead abeam, and in a flat sea. The bigger the enlarge-ment, the more accurate the measurement. The wind speed must be known, and the backstay and runner settings must be recorded for future reference.

However, photographic techniques are not a lot of help when sailing far off-shore or at the height of a tense race when the boat speed seems elusive. The method shown here has much to commend it.

Dark-coloured tapes are stitched vertically to each side of the sail at half height, or where the bend measurement is required. If the bend should be, say, 8 in (200 mm), then the middle of one of the tapes should be that distance back from the luff. The

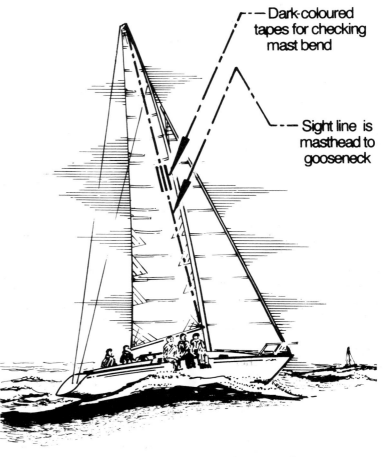

Dark-coloured tapes for checking mast bend

Sight line is masthead to gooseneck

others should be at known intervals.

By sighting up the mast aft edge from the goose-neck, the observer can see if the correct tape is in line with the masthead. This

takes practice, and it is no bad thing to get more than one person to do the sight-ing. Anyone with rain on both sides of their specta-cles is not likely to get a precise sighting.

Learning from creases

Those awkward creases that appear in a mainsail from time to time are useful guides to what is wrong with a sail. The drawing shows the pattern of furrows that results from too much mast bend. This bend has to match the cut of the sail, so if a new sail is hoisted and creases result, then the sailmaker may not have designed his latest product to match the bend in the mast. The rigging has to be readjusted to suit the new mainsail, and this should be done by working with the sailmaker.

If the sailmaker says that the batten tensions are wrong, these are altered first. However, battens must not be too tight in their pockets, otherwise other problems will arise. For instance, when the yacht tacks, all or some of the battens may refuse to reverse their bend across to the new tack, and instead remain bowed out to windward. And nothing ruins the performance of a mainsail like battens curved boldly out to windward.

An old tired mainsail sometimes has heavy creases at the corners, especially at the head and clew, where years of hard work have crinkled the cloth and the sun has hard-

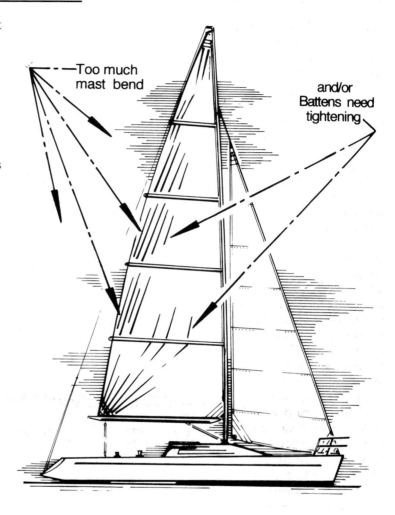

Too much mast bend

and/or Battens need tightening

ened the Terylene/Dacron into permanent ridges at the corners. This is a different problem to the one shown here, which is found in a new or middle-aged sail.

One easy way to eliminate this set of creases is to progressively tighten the battens and/or straighten the curve in the mast. The creases should start to fade as the alterations are made. It helps if the rigging screws are of the type that have graduations, so that their settings can be recorded and subsequently reproduced.

Long-lasting tell-tales

The only way to be sure about the wind flow over a sail is to have plenty of tell-tales. In the course of a season these short lengths of fluttering cloth get worn, torn off and broken, so it is logical to start off with a few extras. Some tell-tales get ripped off the mainsail leech by the backstay, and this can happen in the middle of a race when the sail cannot be lowered for repairs.

There is no universal agreement as to the best type of tell-tale. Pieces of dark-coloured knitting wool are popular, especially if the wool is slightly oily so that it does not soak up rain. However, it is not a lot of use on large yachts, where strips of spinnaker cloth roughly ½ in (12 mm) wide are favoured instead. The length of a tell-tale will generally be about 6 in (15 cm), with roughly ½ in (12 mm) of that length stitched on. For yachts over about 50 ft (15 m), though, these dimensions must be doubled for otherwise the high tell-tales will be too hard to see.

It is normal practice to cut the spinnaker cloth strips with a hot-knife to seal the edges, but enthusiasts use ordinary scissors, and cut the strips before machine-washing them. This results in thin threads teasing out from the edges, so the tell-tales are reputed to be just that tiny bit more efficient in light airs..... there are no lengths to which fanatics will not go for efficiency!

Machine-washing makes the tell-tales pliable and removes any starchiness and chemical 'fillers' in the cloth. It is usual to use off-cuts from a sail loft for the tell-tales, and dark colours are essential. On headsails, the port ones are normally red and the starboard ones are dark green or black.

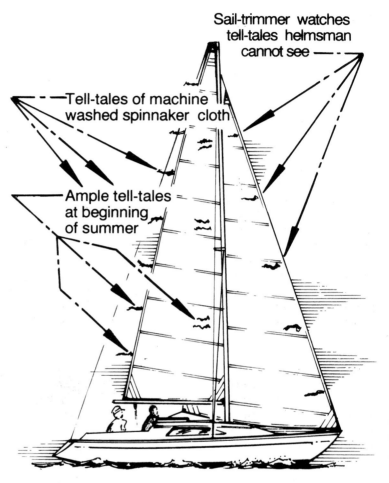

Sail-trimmer watches tell-tales helmsman cannot see — · -

Tell-tales of machine washed spinnaker cloth

Ample tell-tales at beginning of summer

Sail curvature detectors

It can be hard to be sure just what curvature the mainsail has, especially in poor light. Even experienced sailmakers sometimes have trouble assessing exactly where the fullest part of the sail is, and just how much fullness there is.

Two or three dark-coloured tapes sewn horizontally fore-and-aft, on both sides, suddenly make it easy to see the aerofoil shape. Photographs are not much help without these tapes, but with them a few photographs sensibly studied can substantially improve a yacht's performance.

The tapes must be well clear of the numbers and reef eyes. They need not be wide, provided they can be seen even at dusk and in the rain. On small boats, say under 26 ft (8 m), ½ in (12 mm) tapes should be fine. Over that size, 1 in (25 mm) tape will be suitable for yachts up to about 50 ft (15 m).

If the tapes are not run right into the luff and leech (though they should be close), repairs and alterations are easier. Also along the edges of sails there are layers of cloth building up to a considerable thickness in places.

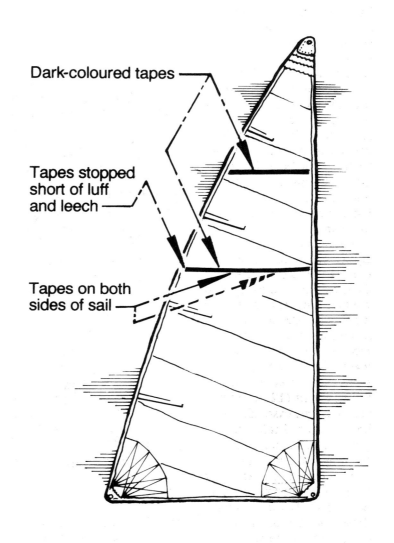

Dark-coloured tapes

Tapes stopped short of luff and leech

Tapes on both sides of sail

Adding even one extra layer each side is something to be discouraged, which is another reason for stopping the tapes just clear of the edges.

Gauging mainsail twist

The amount of twist along the leech of a mainsail affects performance, and in general, needs to be increased in light airs. Also, if there is wind sheer that increases with height, then the sail needs more twist on the starboard tack.

It is not easy to assess just how much twist the mainsail has, especially for beginners, or at night. However, if there is a topping lift, this can be gently tightened until it extends in a straight line from masthead to boom outer end. The distances between it and each batten can then be guessed, and the results written down.

This gives an initial record, so it is easy to repeat these readings on future occasions when the wind and sea conditions are the same. It may help to ask several people to look aloft and agree on the distances to improve accuracy.

A rule taped on to a boathook can sometimes be held aloft to measure the distance between the bottom batten and the topping lift. Given this distance, it is then easier to judge the upper distances.

On many racing yachts there is no topping lift, and here a good ploy is to rig a thin line temporarily between the masthead and boom end. It makes life easier if this line, or the topping lift for that matter, is brightly coloured.

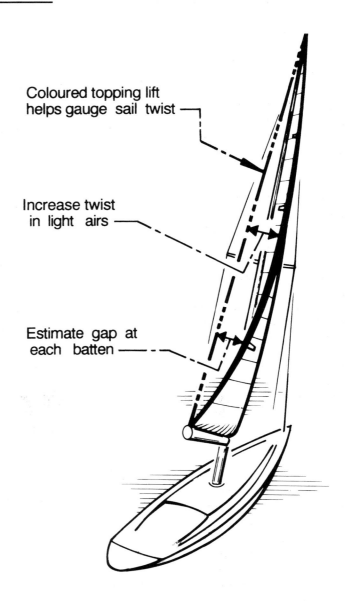

Coloured topping lift helps gauge sail twist

Increase twist in light airs

Estimate gap at each batten

Batten variations

Sailmakers do not always supply the correct battens for a particular mainsail. Makers of One-design sails, for instance, supply identical battens with all sails made for the same class, even though, generally speaking, battens used in northern climates need to be slightly stiffer than those in warmer, gentler conditions.

It is not easy to get the battens to work perfectly in all wind conditions. Keen crews change battens to suit light or strong breezes, and experiment to get just the right sail cambers at different levels.

Broadly speaking, the top batten needs to be the lightest and most flexible. The bottom one may have to cope with harsh handling during reefing, therefore it has to be strong. It does not need to bend much, so the batten can be slightly too tough and stiff without noticeable loss of performance.

If a batten is too stiff it can often be thinned down in width or depth. This work should be done gradually, with plenty of trial sailing between each modification. Battens that are too floppy can be stiffened by adding extra layers of glassfibre; this is seldom

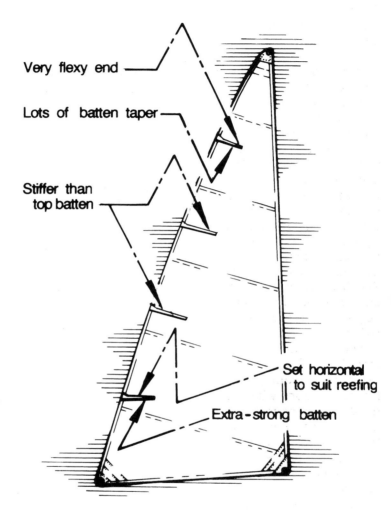

Very flexy end

Lots of batten taper

Stiffer than top batten

Set horizontal to suit reefing

Extra-strong batten

worthwhile, though, and it is better to buy thicker or stiffer battens, and keep the old ones as spares or for different wind strengths.

In the days of wooden battens, sometimes holes were drilled to increase the flexibility, but this was never as good as varying the thickness or depth, or both. Drilling holes in glassfibre battens is not recommended.

Headboards for racing fanatics

No one wants excess weight on a boat, and the worst place for this is at the masthead. For crew who like to cut out every particle of poundage, the mainsail headboard offers opportunities. The headboard is in two identical pieces which are secured port and starboard, right at the top of the sail.

When ordering a new sail, it is essential to get hold of the headboard panels from the sailmaker before he starts to assemble the sail, and his advice should be sought before the work on the headboard begins. On some boats headboard modifications are not allowed by the class rules.

The headboard has a hole through the top forward corner which takes the main halyard, and the board distributes the loading on to the sail. So as long as there is just sufficient area and strength in the board, everything will be fine – except that an accident or lack of maintenance may ruin the best laid plans.

Most boards are made with a good factor of safety and they are deeper than they need to be. If the bottom quarter – or even bottom third – is cut away

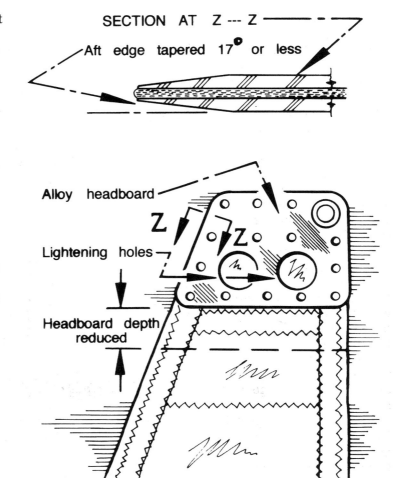

(provided plenty of rivets are put through), the board should still work well in normal racing conditions.

The area of material between the rivets need not be extensive, so long as there is no risk that the board will buckle or fracture when highly stressed. A conservative pattern of

lightening holes is normally acceptable, especially in the bottom half of the headboard.

The trailing edge of the headboard should be faired away so that wind burbling in the wake is reduced. A faired-off angle of 17° is needed, and of course all rivets need countersinking.

'Dutchman' controls mainsail

This clever but simple invention gives control over mainsails in all weathers. A 'Dutchman' is a set of two or more thin vertical ropes extending down from a fixed-length permanently set-up topping lift to the top of the boom. These vertical lines pass through holes in plastic 'plates' secured to the sail. The 'plates' prevent the sail wearing locally and keep it exactly in position.

As the sail is lowered it folds itself in neat zig-zags on the boom. If the sail is being reefed, again it settles in a good-tempered way on top of the boom without thrashing about out of control. During the unreefing process, the sail remains docile and does not go wild and lash about.

A few sailmakers specialise in fitting 'Dutchmen', and it is best to consult them when going for this apparently simple gadget because the vertical lines must be slightly curved and great care is needed to keep ropes clear of the crosstrees, where they may get caught round the back when the sail is square off, on the run.

The sort of people who particularly like this gadget are singlehanded sailors, long-range voyagers, and

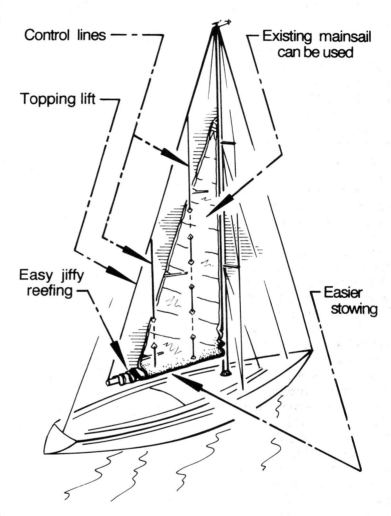

Control lines

Topping lift

Easy jiffy reefing

Existing mainsail can be used

Easier stowing

anyone feeling the effects of advancing years or creaking joints. On a yacht where the mainsail is over the magic 500 sq ft (46 sq m), which is the biggest area

that the average, fit, experienced person can manage in all weathers, this gadget is a great boon. It can be fitted on new or old sails, and on mizzens.

'Dutchman' for an old sail

The advantages of having a 'Dutchman' on a mainsail are so great that owners ask for old sails to be equipped with this convenient stowage-and-control device. However, the price of the parts and the cost of having a sailmaker fit them are such that the disadvantages have also to be considered.

First, there is almost bound to be a little extra chafe; maybe not much, but from small defects larger ones flow. Also, the new vertical lines will foul the crosstrees if the 'Dutchman' is not properly tailored to fit the rig.

The plain fact is that an old mainsail that has only a couple of years of safe sailing left in it should not be fitted with a 'Dutchman' unless there are some rather special reasons. Before any decision is made to fit a 'Dutchman', the sail should be carefully assessed, first to ensure that there is plenty of life left in it, and secondly, to check that existing components, like the reef points, are compatible with the new equipment. Of course, the reef points can be reduced in number, perhaps by eliminating alternate ones, or by making new widely spaced ones. However, this involves extra expenditure.

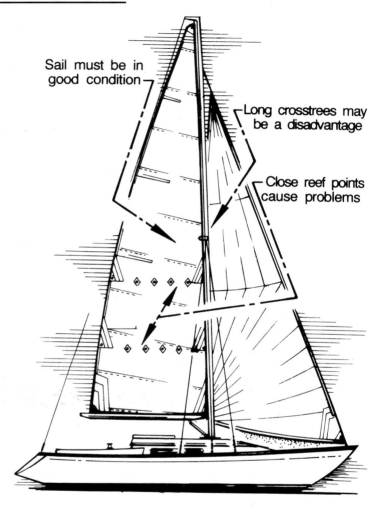

Sail must be in good condition

Long crosstrees may be a disadvantage

Close reef points cause problems

It is sometimes possible to shorten the crosstrees if there is a problem here. As a basic rule, the angle between the side of the mast and the shrouds should not be less than 13° for a cruiser. It *can* be less, but if it is more the mast stresses are reduced.

By measuring the distance from where the upper shroud meets the mast to the crosstree, and the length of the crosstree, the angle can be calculated. It makes sense to ask a mastmaker about the advisability of shortening the crosstrees before doing the job.

Light air sailing

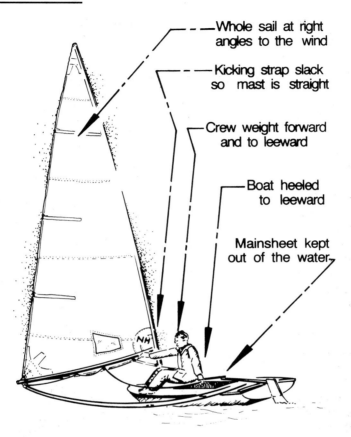

Whole sail at right angles to the wind

Kicking strap slack so mast is straight

Crew weight forward and to leeward

Boat heeled to leeward

Mainsheet kept out of the water

When there is a shortage of wind it has to be used as efficiently as possible. This means presenting the largest possible area of sail to the oncoming air, so as to grab as much passing energy as the sail can take. The kicking strap is kept slack, so that the mast is straight and the sail is not made unnecessarily baggy.

The minimum drag from the hull is obtained by keeping the transom well out of the water and the immersed part of the hull shell as small in area as possible. This reduces skin friction, which is all-important when the boat is going so slowly that there is no 'wave-making' resistance.

The crew move gently forward and to leeward. All movements are careful and unhurried so that the mast is never shaken nor the wind flow over the sail disturbed. It can be awkward to steer from this forward position, and a useful gadget is a lock on the tiller extension pivot. With the universal joint clamped tight, the extension acts like a rigid addition on the fore end of the tiller.

Though the drawing shows a small dinghy, all these principles apply to larger boats.

Easier reefing

On some yachts, notably offshore cruisers, the reef pennants are kept permanently in position, led through the leech eyes. This means that if the reef has to be hauled down in a hurry, the equipment is all ready. However, it also means that the pennants chafe continuously, and also detract a little from the sail's efficiency.

A racing crew does not want anything to spoil the flow of the wind over the sail, so on racing craft the pennants are not rove off through the leech eyes till they are needed. This job can be very difficult, especially on a mainsail where the eye is out of reach until the sail has been lowered. Once lowered, the leech thrashes about, so getting the pennant through the eye is still difficult.

'Runner' lines, sometimes called 'leaders', make life much easier. They are thin, continuous ropes led through the clew eye and up to a reef eye then back to the clew, with a 'cut' splice kept near the bottom.

When a reef pennant has to be put in position, its end is tucked through the cut splice, and probably wrapped round and back through the splice for extra security. The runner line is pulled on the back of the sail and this conveys the pennant up, through the reef eye and back down to the boom.

It is important that the cut splice is not too large, and this can be found out by experimenting. To begin with, a splice length of 1 in (25 mm) for every 13 ft (4 m) of yacht length should be tried.

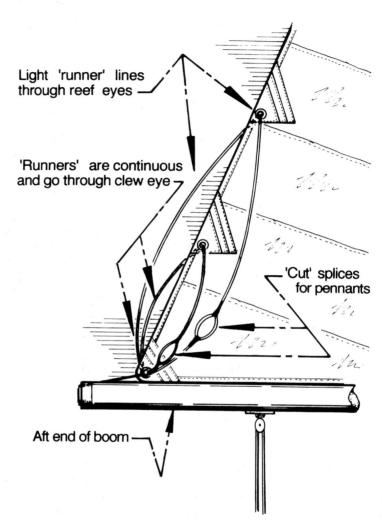

Light 'runner' lines through reef eyes

'Runners' are continuous and go through clew eye

'Cut' splices for pennants

Aft end of boom

Safer reefing

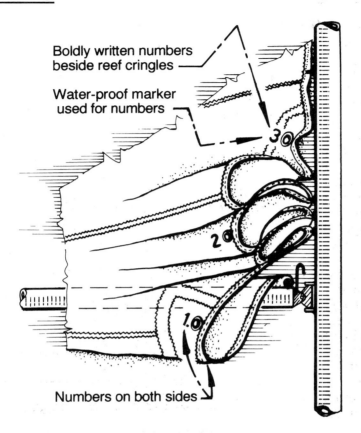

Boldly written numbers beside reef cringles ⸻

Water-proof marker used for numbers ⸺

Numbers on both sides ⤵

When putting a jiffy reef in the mainsail, there are times when it is easy to get the wrong luff cringle hooked on by the gooseneck. For instance, when the reef is being put in before hoisting the sail, there is a great mass of sail bunched near the mast, and even experienced crew get the wrong eye hooked on. In the dark, or in seriously bad weather, the job is even more difficult.

It only takes a minute to mark the eyes with their correct numbers, starting from the bottom. It may not be enough to mark the sail on both sides because the numbers may not show up in the dark. To get round this, a single turn of light line is knotted through the No 1 reef eye, two turns through the No 2 eye, and so on. These pieces of line are easily felt, even in adverse conditions.

To be doubly safe, the leech eyes should also be numbered, though it is less likely that they will be muddled up. However, tired seasick people can make amazing mistakes, so the few minutes spent marking all the reef cringles may pay off one bleak rough night. Racing owners need no urging to take this sort of precaution, because they know races are won and lost by such small details.

Swift unreefing

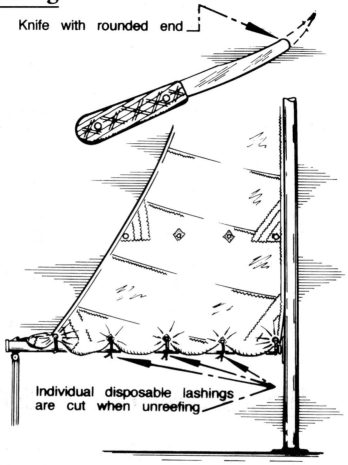

Knife with rounded end

Individual disposable lashings
are cut when unreefing

When the time comes to take out a reef the sea state is often rough, with the leftover dregs of a gale still stirring things up. The crew are tired and liable to make mistakes, so anything that simplifies life is welcome.

Instead of having a row of lashings that have to be untied at each reef point, it is easier to have disposable lengths of light (but adequate) thin rope which is slashed through with a knife. It is important not to damage the sail, so the knife used must have a rounded end to its blade, as shown in the enlarged drawing at the top of the page. This round blade end is made by grinding on an electric grind-stone, or by cutting and filing.

Whenever a reef is being taken out it is essential to release the reef points before slackening off either the luff or leech reef eyes. As a safety precaution, some owners have quite thin lines through the reef points, so that if by accident one of the main pennants is released first, the lashings at the points burst before the sail tears.

Keep a knife handy on deck

Cut reef points to save sail

Pennant let go too soon

If you wander down the marina walkways during a major regatta, you will see a sheath knife on the back of the mast or on the solid kicking strap or vang on quite a few of the top boats. This is for cutting the vang line in an emergency, or any other rope that is jammed and urgently needs releasing.

When undoing a slab reef as the weather improves, it is important to undo the reef points *first*. Yet sometimes the crew are tired or

inexperienced, or it is dark, or there is a lack of co-ordination, and the aft pennant is slackened off before the reef points.

There is no time to retighten the pennant. Someone must instantly slash through the reef points starting from the aft end to prevent the sail ripping. It is essential not to carve a slice out of the sail in the general excitement. If the knife blade is slipped between the boom and the

reef point and cut downwards, all should go well.

The knife must be sharp, and the reef points need not be massive: they are only needed to keep the sail neatly bundled up and not thrashing about in the strong wind. They are almost always of secondary importance, and on some sails the first reef line does not even have reef points or eyelets to fit them.

Steadying sail for all seasons

It is common for a steadying sail to be left up all through a voyage, even when the wind is from dead ahead, so that the sail is not working, just flapping. Also, this sail has to survive bad weather as well as much slatting, so it is logical to have it fully battened.

However, battens that extend right across a sail need special slides and cause troubles at the fore end of the pockets. This is why it is suggested that the battens should be almost, but not quite, full length. Long battens usually cause a lot of batten pocket wear, which explains the importance of plastic tubing on the shrouds. They act like rollers and are softer as well as smoother than rigging wire.

Lazyjacks also cause wear on the pockets, but this form of topping lift-cum-sail controller is well worth having, especially on a boat with a small or light crew. As the sail comes down, it largely stows itself and does not flop on deck.

Any boat that has a steadying sail is likely to be steered from inside a wheelhouse, and the sheet(s) should be handy so that no one has to go out in the wet to adjust the ropes.

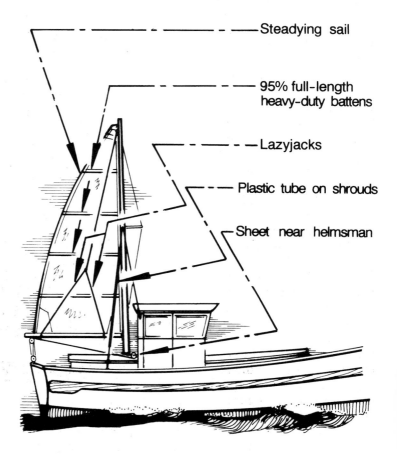

Steadying sail

95% full-length heavy-duty battens

Lazyjacks

Plastic tube on shrouds

Sheet near helmsman

If ever there was a good case for having extra-heavy sail-cloth, this is it. Larger corners than usual also make sense. Some owners like to have a reef or two; others say they just take the sail down when the weather gets boisterous.

2. Genoas

Measuring for a new headsail

When no accurate sail plan is available, it is not difficult to get the measurements for a new headsail from a yacht. Two pieces of pre-stretched terylene or dacron rope, well over the length of the luff, are tied to the headsail halyard shackle. They are hauled aloft until the shackle is in the normal 'sailing' position. Typically this will be very roughly 3 per cent of the luff length down the forestay from the halyard sheave for a full-height cruising genoa.

It may be difficult to locate the head of the sail correctly so here is a work-able procedure. Haul the halyard up tight to its limit with the shackle jammed on the sheave and the luff rope attached. Next pull the luff rope back down the 3 per cent. An intelligent guess as to what the length of the luff is has sometimes to be taken. To get this more accurate ask three people to make the guess then take the average of their 'guesstimates'.

The rope representing the luff of the new sail, labelled '1st rope', is pulled down to the deck. A knot is made where the tack will be and the rope is then secured in position.

The 2nd rope, which shows the line of the leech,

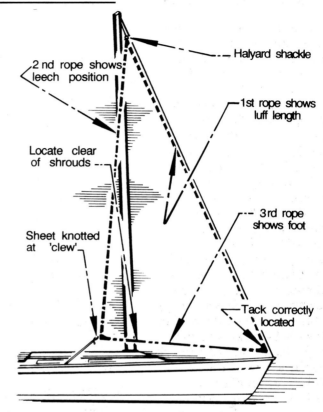

is taken down to the clew location and knotted here, then fixed in place. The third rope is knotted at tack and clew. This is the foot of the new sail but without any 'droop'. A fourth rope can be tied loosely to show the line and the depth of the 'droop' if required.

With all ropes in position, an inspection from well out-board is strongly recom-mended. Also check the sheet lead to the genoa car.

It is important that the sail clears the shrouds and crosstrees, so it may be necessary to move the clew forward, or have a hollow cut in the leech.

Once the three ropes are correctly positioned, the headsail halyard is lowered and the three ropes are carefully measured, keeping them at the same tension as when they were aloft. When sail-makers go through this whole procedure they use three tape measures which speeds the job up and solves the problem of rope stretch.

Limitation of sailhead height

In theory, it makes sense to design the top of a headsail at the top of the forestay, because this will give the maximum area. However, a sail made as long as this on the luff will press against the lee side of the mast at the top, and below this the main will be backwinded. The air flow on the wind-ward side of the sail will not follow the sail, but will bend awkwardly round the windward side of the mast – as shown in the drawing.

This crinkled air stream is inefficient, and has to be avoided by lowering the head of the sail when drawing the sail plan. The problem is, by how much should the head of the sail be brought down? The John Illingworth formula is a handy starting point for genoas:

C = 0.016 x I x U x O – 0.5h

where
C = The clearance between the sail head and the top of the stay
I = Height of the triangle
U = Maximum wind strength on the Beaufort Scale, for which the sail is designed when beating
O = Overlap ratio. This assumes that a perpend-icular is dropped from the clew, and the distance measured from the tack

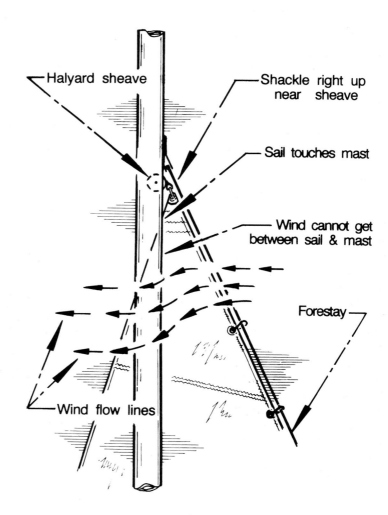

Halyard sheave

Shackle right up near sheave

Sail touches mast

Wind cannot get between sail & mast

Forestay

Wind flow lines

back to that base point. If a sail has a 15 ft long foot, and the base of the fore-triangle is 10 ft then the overlap ratio is 1.5
h = The hollow of the leech. **All dimensions in feet and decimals of a foot**.

It can be argued that this formula is dated, but it has the great advantage of sim-plicity and convenience; personal experience will provide data to adjust it.

Sails for in-cabin steering

When the steering position is down below, the helmsman has limited vision. As he cannot nip up on deck at frequent intervals to look round, it is essential that the sails do not hide much of the horizon from him.

A high-cut headsail with its tack well off the deck is needed. If roller furling gear is fitted, the drum will keep the tack some distance off the deck, but it may be best to raise the drum up to the top of the pulpit. This ensures a view under the sail even when the yacht is heeled.

The location of the tell-tales will have to be adjusted to suit the helmsman's line of sight, and it may be worthwhile fitting a Windex on a short portable bowsprit. It may even pay to have a pair of them, off-set port and starboard ahead of the bow, to show the wind direction. Properly arranged, they can be quickly taken in before coming into a marina or moorings.

Seeing to leeward is a problem in lots of yachts, but if there is a roller furling genoa, it can quickly be reduced in area..... as fast as the wind increases. This will keep the angle of heel to an acceptable level and let the helmsman see

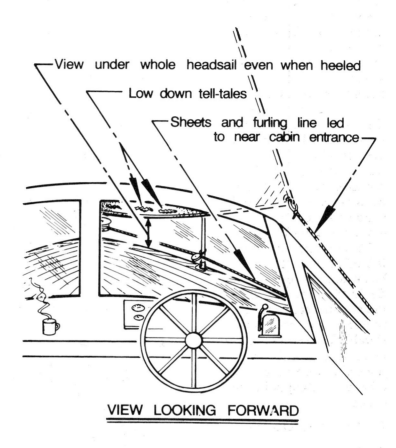

View under whole headsail even when heeled

Low down tell-tales

Sheets and furling line led to near cabin entrance

VIEW LOOKING FORWARD

what is going to hit him next. However, the furling line must be close to hand, and ideally led right to the steering position. If it is not in the cabin, it has to be close to the entrance.

The same applies to the genoa sheets, since they will need trimming as often as

the furling line. It may pay to shift the sheet winches so that the helmsman can work them while he is still close to the steering wheel.

Smooth headsail hoisting

Sometimes a headsail refuses to glide smoothly up the luff foil, in spite of energetic work on the halyard. If the sail is bunched too far aft on the foredeck it has an awkward journey, with a sharp turn at the pre-feeder, so jamming may occur.

If only the very top of the sail has been entered in the luff groove, the head may twist and jam. Once the sail has been entered, a slight but continuous tension should be kept on the halyard.

Ideally the luff should be neatly zig-zagged just behind the forestay. If the sail has to be left in that location for some time, perhaps while the race committee are trying to establish a good starting line, then a sail tier, or even several of them, will be needed to keep everything in the correct position.

When the sheets are not completely slack, the middle or lower part of the luff may not be able to slither into the pre-feeder effortlessly. However, no-one wants to grab in miles of rope when sheeting in, so the amount of slackness needs to be assessed intelligently.

Of course, if the luff tape is tatty there may be

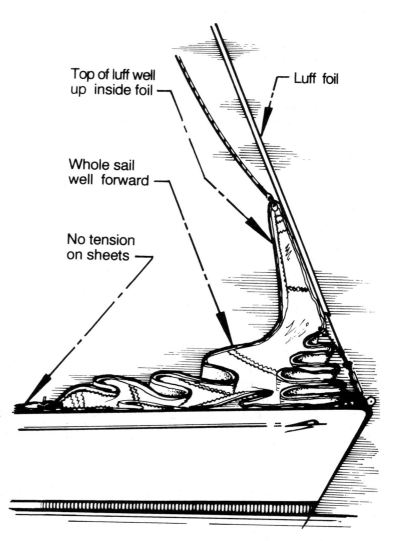

Top of luff well up inside foil

Luff foil

Whole sail well forward

No tension on sheets

trouble, whatever precautions are taken by the foredeck hand. Tapes chafe without being noticed, especially right at the top, and if a genoa is well used for a whole season, it may need at least minor repairs before the end of the summer.

Creases low on the luff

What happens if the head-sail halyard is tight up, yet there are horizontal creases running aft from the fore-stay, low down on the luff? It may be that the halyard winch is not powerful enough to tighten the luff, or there is too much friction in the luff foil, or the crew may be short of muscle.

The obvious way round the problem is to arrange for the tack to be hauled downwards. This can be done with a tackle, or a winch, or even a combination of these. On some craft there is an anchor windlass on the foredeck that can be used.

If there is a shortage of space under the tack, it may be necessary to fit a block on the side of the sail. Using one of the special 'cheek' blocks specially made for securing on to sails with stitched tapes, the tack can be brought right down to the deck. However, this type of block has a single sheave, so it will only give a two-to-one purchase. This is hardly likely to be enough, so it is almost certainly going to be necessary to have another tackle extending aft along the deck, or to lead the downhaul to a winch.

On some craft the best technique will be to lead the downhaul back to a winch by the cockpit. It is often possible to do this using blocks secured to the stanchion bases. This is the way roller furling lines are led aft and kept clear of the walking area on the sidedeck.

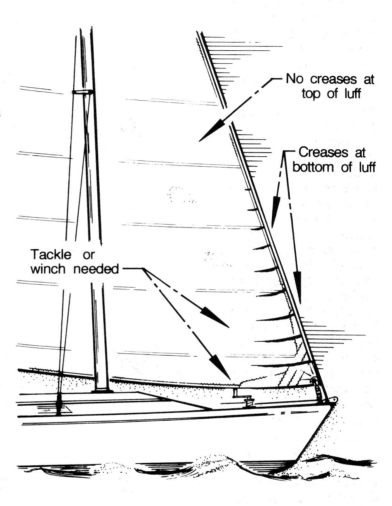

No creases at top of luff

Creases at bottom of luff

Tackle or winch needed

Sheeting an extra-large headsail

As a rough rule, a genoa with a foot much over 1.5 times the length between the tack-down point and the mast is not effective because it is impossible to sheet correctly. The area along the leech tends to backwind the mainsail, especially when going to windward.

However, there is nothing like adding sail area to get a yacht going well. So here is a ploy to get the sheet lead outboard from the deck edge that works well on a reach and in light airs.

The sheet goes through a snatch block rigged from the boom end, or near the end. This block needs to be on an outhaul so that the sheet can be clipped in by a crew on the sidedeck. Before tacking, the sheet has to be freed from the block and either the same sheet led round the mast and back into the snatch block, or a second sheet made ready, and secured in the block as the yacht settles on the new tack.

Clearly this is not a rig for short tacking, and it is not often seen, except on long-range cruisers. Such craft seldom tack, and go to windward as little as can be managed by taking established downwind routes.

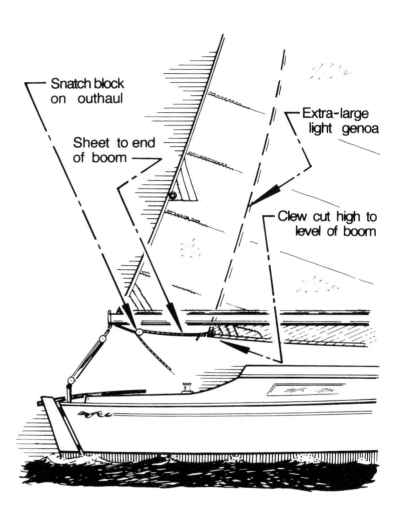

Most rating rules penalise very long-footed headsails, but in the right conditions this sheeting arrangement has much to commend it. Asymmetrical spinnakers, reaching genoas, ballooners, and many of those special reaching and downwind headsails given their own 'company' names by sail-making firms, can benefit from this sheeting technique.

To be safe, the gear must not be flimsy, and all ropes must run freely.

Judging headsail sheeting

If a boat is going well, the crew want to be able to repeat the settings of the halyards, sheets, and so on next time they encounter the same wind speed and sea conditions. It is easy enough to put a genoa sheet lead back to a particular location on the track, but getting the sheet tension the same, time after time, can be more difficult.

One good measure is the distance off the crosstree end of the headsail leech. Once it has been established that for, say, force 3 the genoa should be 4 in (100 mm) off the crosstree, all the crew have to do is to sheet in the same amount each time. The problem comes down to judging the distance off the crosstree tip from the relatively far-away cockpit. To help with this, a series of marks on the crosstrees can be a wonderful aid.

Brightly coloured plastic tape or paint marks can be used, and it will normally be necessary to have at least three marks. Each mark must be bright enough to be easily seen at dusk. As a rough guide, the coloured bands should be 1 in (25 mm) wide for every 20 ft (6 m) of yacht length. The gaps between should be about three times the width

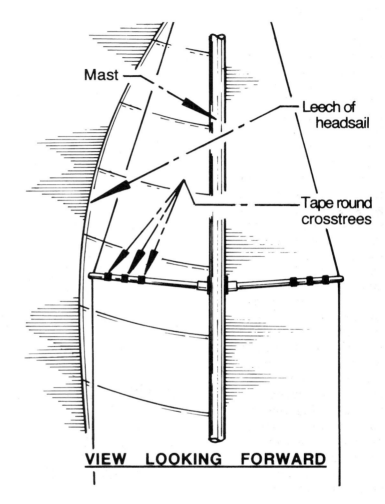

Mast

Leech of headsail

Tape round crosstrees

VIEW LOOKING FORWARD

of the coloured bands.

In the drawing, the leech has been sheeted in until it is 75 per cent of the gap between two colour bands, off the end of the crosstree. The beauty of this scheme is that the coloured bands on

the crosstrees can be put on at the beginning of the season, before the correct sheeting tensions are known. Subsequent experience will build up a data base of correct 'distances off the crosstrees'.

Sheeting when reaching

Using a Barber hauler when the yacht is no longer fully close-hauled is a well-established technique. The headsail sheet has to be slackened off from the position used for going to windward, but merely easing the sheet is not enough. The direction of pull of the sheet needs to be further outboard, so that the leech of the sail goes further off the yacht's centreline, and the wind is deflected further outboard.

A simple arrangement consists of a block shackled to the toerail, with a second sheet led from the clew of the sail through this newly sited block and back to the cockpit. In any weight of wind the sheet winch normally used for the spinnaker sheets and guys can be used for a Barber hauler.

Of course there are times and situations where the Barber hauler needs to lead inboard, for instance on cruisers with unsophisticated sheet leads. In light airs a Barber hauler block can be secured to a cabin-top hand rail, but this is risky. Hand rails are usually designed to take loads of below 200 lb (100 kg), and anything above this is liable to result in serious damage.

Sometimes the only way to organise an *inward*

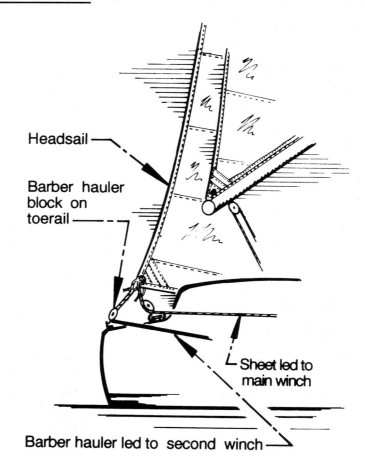

Headsail

Barber hauler block on toerail

Sheet led to main winch

Barber hauler led to second winch

tension is to tie a block to a length of line leading right across the cabin top, and fixed to the windward toerail. This needs care, especially as it is liable to cause the crew going forward to trip. Also, the height of the cabin top may result in a block position and lead that is too high.

Heavy weather downwind

There comes a time, as the wind rises from strong to worrying, when sensible crews realise that they can no longer carry a spinnaker. The safe alternative is a headsail, held right out on the opposite side to the mainsail by the spinnaker pole.

There are different techniques for arranging this 'wung out' jib, but the following procedure has the virtues of simplicity and safety.

With the sail sheeted in on the port side the starboard sheet is led through the outer end of the spinnaker boom, or a block on the outer end of this boom. The boom is clipped on to the mast, and lifted with a halyard. A fore guy and an aft guy are secured to the outer end of the pole, and the pole is then swung outboard and secured tightly. As these guys lead downwards, in theory it is not necessary to have a spinnaker pole downhaul, but many people fit one for safety.

The headsail is hauled to starboard using the sheet through the pole end. This sheet is tightened till the sail is pulling well, then the height and location of the outer end of the spinnaker pole is adjusted

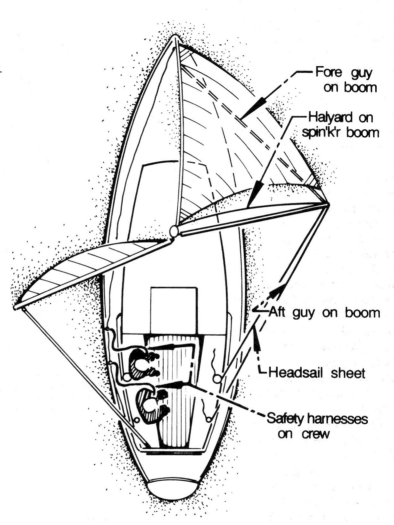

— Fore guy on boom

— Halyard on spin'k'r boom

— Aft guy on boom

— Headsail sheet

— Safety harnesses on crew

so that it is close to the foresail clew.

A disadvantage of this rig is that it takes time to reverse the process, so no one should fall overboard,

especially as the weather will usually be bad when this rig is used. Therefore all the crew must have permanently secured safety harnesses.

Roller furling problems

Though there are lots of different makes of roller furling gear, many of them share a problem. This relates to the top swivel, which has to be restrained from rotating when the sail is being rolled up. On some there is a special 'stop' that prevents the swivel rotating.

A more common solution is to have the halyard (which is secured to the top swivel) diverted away from the line of the forestay, as shown in the drawing. The angle at which it leads has to be between 20° and 30°. Anything less and the halyard may get wrapped round the forestay; anything more and there can be a problem getting the swivel right up.

The halyard is led through a block or roller on the fore side of the mast to get the angle right. Sometimes, to save money, there is just an eye plate through which the halyard goes, but on anything except a small boat this tends to increase the friction on the halyard to an unacceptable level.

When fitting the 'diverter' block it may pay to have a pair of templates made up, using cardboard or scrap plywood. They will be simple triangles, one with an angle of 20°, and the

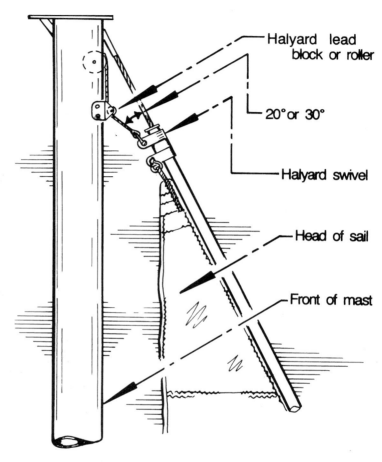

Halyard lead block or roller

20° or 30°

Halyard swivel

Head of sail

Front of mast

other with an angle of 30°. With this method, the location of the lead block can be made precisely right.

The block sometimes has to stand up to big loads, so it should ideally be bolted in place, even though this means removing the mast-head fitting. Where this top fitting is welded in place, the block will have to be secured with self-tapping screws or rivets. The screws or rivets must be large ones, with a minimum of six fastenings.

Lead of roller furling line

It can be hard work rolling up a furling headsail. Often a winch is used, but the line must be thin to fit on the furler drum, and it is important not to over-strain it. Also an aft winch is usually the one selected for this job, and it is normally quite small.

One way to keep down the friction, and hence the loads, is to have the minimum number of lead blocks between the furling drum and the cockpit. As the whole point of having headsail furling gear is to limit the number of times the crew have to go forward at sea, it is no great disadvantage if the furling line slightly obstructs one sidedeck. As a result, it is seldom necessary to have a lead block at every stanchion.

Just as important, the blocks should not be tiny ones, just because the line is thin. Normally the size of a block is dictated by the diameter of the rope that goes through it. Here it is better to have a block one or two sizes larger than the line would normally require. But, above all, the blocks should have ball bearings or roller bearings to minimise friction. They should also be washed through every few months,

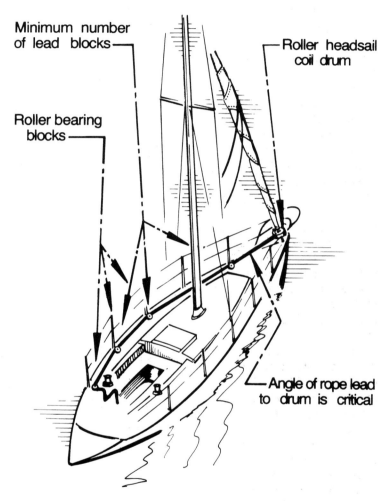

Minimum number of lead blocks

Roller bearing blocks

Roller headsail coil drum

Angle of rope lead to drum is critical

especially if the yacht has been out in rough conditions or is kept in a dusty marina.

Finally, the rope must lead on to the drum at precisely the angle specified by the makers. This means locating the forward block accurately.

Neat roller furling

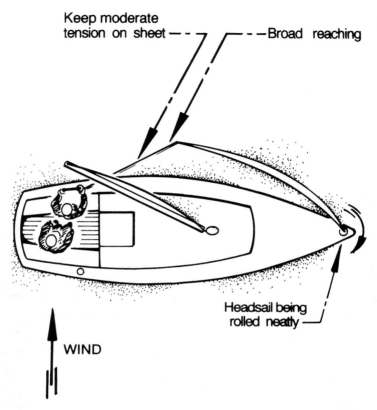

Keep moderate tension on sheet — - —Broad reaching

WIND

Headsail being rolled neatly —

If a roller furling headsail is not neatly stowed, it presents extra windage – and this could be serious in a gale. A bad stow also affects the way a sail wears and weathers, especially if the furling is so untidy that the ultra-violet protection strip no longer covers the whole exposed area. An exceptionally poor wrapping may make the work of hauling in the roller line extremely hard.

There are various techniques for getting a good furl, and the best advice is to do the job before the wind gets too strong. On the average coastal cruiser the sail should be fully wrapped round the forestay before the wind is up to force 7.

To do an ordinary furl when coming into moorings, the yacht should be put on a broad reach. A moderate tension is kept on the lee sheet, but the weather one must be slack. The lee sheet is paid out progressively as the furling line is hauled in.

It is better to keep a steady tension on the furling line rather than give it a series of jerks. If it jams, the first thing to do is see where the blockage occurs, and not try to force the haul-in line to come aft by excessive use of a winch.

Occasionally the furling line gets buried under coils on the drum and may need undoing by hand, each turn being taken off at the drum. Sometimes the slack of the furling line catches round something like an anchor stowed forward.

3. Working Jibs and Staysails

Securing headsail tacks

At the bottom of many forestays there is a pair of simple metal hooks to hold the tack of the headsail. They work well once the sail is aloft, but until the luff has been hauled up tight, the tack eye is liable to drop off the hook.

This means that whoever is hoisting the sail has to send someone else right up to the bow, to hold the sail on the hook till the halyard is secured. On a short-handed yacht there may not be anyone to spare for this job. On a racing boat, the performance will suffer while there is someone right forward upsetting the trim and slowing the upward swoop of the bow as a wave gets under it, which further reduces the speed.

The answer is a simple length of shock cord, made fast to something above the hook such as the lower rail of the pulpit. The loop on the bottom of the shock cord is taken off the hook, the sail tack put on, and finally the shock cord loop replaced. On a big boat the shock cord may have to be thick, or strengthened by the use of several lengths tied together for extra tension.

This idea can be used on the reefing hooks by the gooseneck, or wherever a sail has to be held in a temporary way. Some experimenting may be needed to get the right size of shock cord. Also, this rubbery material perishes as a result of exposure to the sun; it then loses strength and needs replacing.

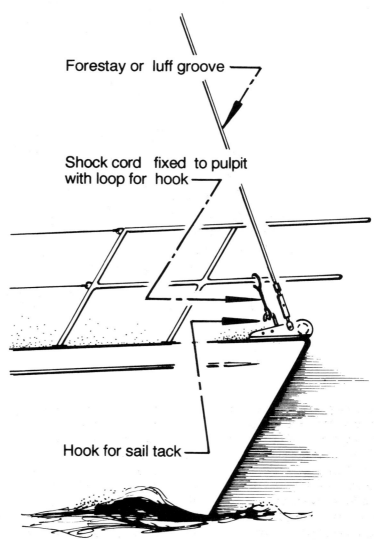

Forestay or luff groove

Shock cord fixed to pulpit with loop for hook

Hook for sail tack

Headsail hank wear

Bronze headsail hanks wear faster than stainless steel ones. Cheap brass ones are quite soft and may get a chafe groove at the top end within a couple of years. This form of wear is shown in the enlarged drawing, top right.

The top hank has to travel right up the forestay and down again each time the sail is hoisted, whereas the bottom one has only a short distance to travel, so the latter hardly wears at all. Careful owners swop the top hank for the bottom one, and the second top one for the one above the bottom one to spread the wear evenly.

The type of hank that is quick and easy to fit, and is popular with sailmakers, has a metal 'tail' that goes through the eye in the sail and is then hammered closed. This 'tail' does not wear out, whereas sewn-on hanks wear badly at the thread that secures them to the sail. However, metal 'tails' cannot usually be opened and reused.

Over the years normal stitched lashings have got a bad reputation for withstanding wear, so good sailmakers fix on hanks with a short length of tough tape, which is wrapped more than once through the eye

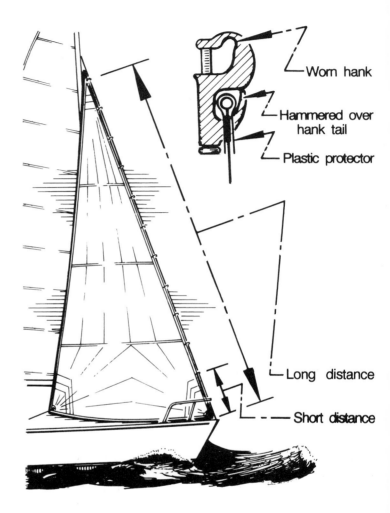

on the sail and the eye on the hank. It is then stitched through to stop the tape unwrapping.

Whatever type of hank is used, thin plastic luff protectors, shown in the enlarged drawing (top right), should always be fitted as they stop wear at a notorious weak spot, namely the cloth round the luff of the sail.

Heavy weather headsail

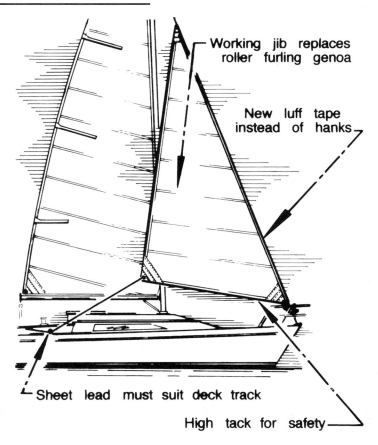

Working jib replaces roller furling genoa

New luff tape instead of hanks

Sheet lead must suit deck track

High tack for safety

A roller furling genoa does a vast amount of work each year, because it is normally the only sail used forward of the mast, apart from the spinnaker and storm jib. Plenty of owners have an old working jib at home, still with its hanks on... a reminder of the time before the yacht was fitted with roller furling gear.

This working jib (provided it is in reasonable condition) can be converted to fit the roller furling equipment, and it can serve various purposes. For instance, if the yacht is setting out in rough weather, this sail is put on the luff foil after the genoa has been taken off. If the yacht is large and the crew few, or not tough, this sail will be easier to handle compared with a full-sized genoa. It will give peace of mind and be less hard work, without much loss of speed.

At the beginning and end of the season when high winds are expected, or when there are beginners on board, having this sail instead of a genoa as the headsail always in use makes a lot of sense. It is easier to roll up and unfurl. When fully furled it presents less windage, and all the time it is saving wear and tear on the genoa, which will last longer as a result.

High-efficiency headsail for short-handed racing

There are a lot of long-distance racing yachts that make use of roller furling headsails; sometimes these roller furlers are on both the inner and outer forestays. This type of sail is certainly easy to handle, because the crew do not leave the cockpit when a decrease or increase in sail area is needed.

However, these sails are not efficient. They suffer from thick luffs as they are rolled up, often have a bad shape when reefed, and when substantially rolled up they cause a lot of adverse windage.

On yachts in the medium and smaller size range there is an alternative that is not often seen, because it requires a tough crew. This is the reefable blade jib. It has two or more reefs that have to be hauled down in the conventional way. However, the sail is always a good shape, and it does not suffer from the bulbous thick luff at any stage. The one shown has tilted reefs to give visibility under the sail and to reduce the chances of a sea filling the foot.

On small boats, the leech reef eyes are located low enough for the crew to reach them while standing on deck. On larger yachts, a

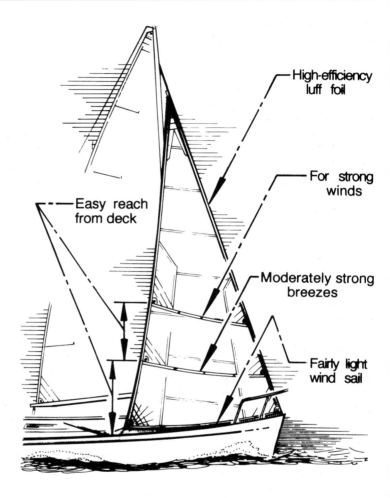

Easy reach from deck

High-efficiency luff foil

For strong winds

Moderately strong breezes

Fairly light wind sail

leading line to thread the reefing pennant through the leech reef eye is used, or the leech reefing pennants are kept permanently rove off. Incidentally, the yacht is kept moving during reefing.

This sail is far cheaper than a roller furling headsail plus the cost of its furl-

ing gear. It is not effective in very light airs, when a ghoster is needed, and in gales a storm jib is required. But in between, this sail can be a low-cost race winner, especially with a hard-working crew who reef and unreef as often as the wind changes demand.

Blade jib

In heavy weather, a sail that looks after itself somewhat is an enormous asset. A blade jib does not chafe on the shrouds because it does not extend far aft sufficiently to touch them; it also needs less fiddling with the leech line because it has battens, which incidentally reduce flogging and hence wear and tear.

Tacking with this sail is quick and easy due to the lack of overlap. With a little co-operation from the helmsman, it is possible to have the sail sheeted in as far as is needed for the beginning of a new tack, before the sail fills properly. Admittedly, once the boat is moving fast again the sail will need retrimming, but that is normal racing practice.

For cruising, this sail might be cut higher at the bottom, perhaps with no 'droop' along the foot, to reduce chafe on the pulpit and guard rail wires and to give a better view forward. The lower battens might be even longer to minimise flogging when hoisting or tacking, and so further reduce wear.

This sail needs to be strong since it is only set in bad weather, or when cruising short-handed; in the latter case, one wants a

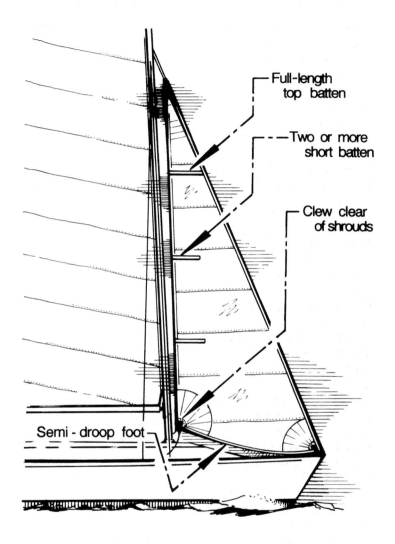

sail that is going to give absolutely no trouble even in a gale..... so triple stitching makes double sense.

If this sail is hanked on, the hanks should be one

size larger than normal, and made of stainless steel, not bronze. The latter wears too fast and is liable to seize when stowed away wet for a long period.

Wind increase adjustment

This technique can be used on some No 2 genoas, but is mainly used on No 3 genoas and working jibs. It consists of slackening the halyard and hauling down the tack.

Lowering a headsail down the forestay, without making other changes, can have beneficial effects when there is an increase in the wind speed. Apart from changes in the sail's curvature, it lowers the centre of effort, and so reduces the heeling moment.

Lowering a sail's working position is not always easy – or even possible. However, if the sail has a tack pennant this can be shortened or taken right away, and the sail clipped right down on deck. Likewise, if the tack has been at the top of the rigging screw, it is often possible to shift it down to deck level.

One effect of lowering the sail is to open up the top of the leech, if the lead block is not moved. This reduces back-winding on the mainsail, and lowers the side pressure high up on the headsail. It is the equivalent to moving the lead block aft to tighten the tension along the foot of the sail. As the sail is

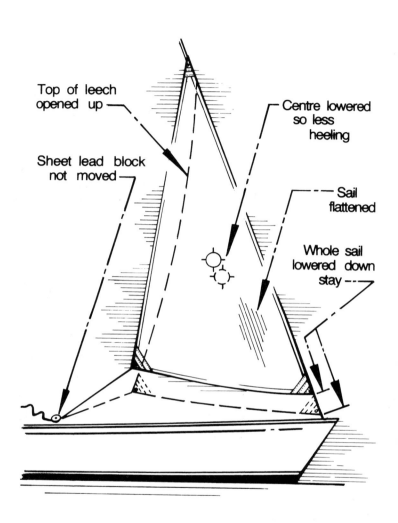

Top of leech opened up —

Sheet lead block not moved —

Centre lowered so less heeling

Sail flattened

Whole sail lowered down stay ---

moving down, it is also going forward slightly, because the forestay is raked. This means that as well as tightening the foot, the sail is in effect flattened by the sheet.

Staysail under spinnaker

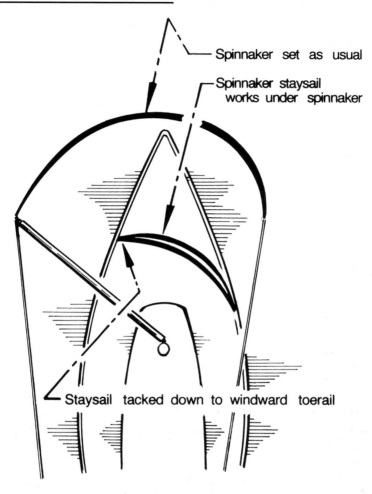

Spinnaker set as usual

Spinnaker staysail
works under spinnaker

Staysail tacked down to windward toerail

When up and flying, spin-nakers do not extend any-where near the deck, so a lot of wind escapes beneath the foot of the sail. Spin-naker staysails are designed to use this otherwise wasted air flow to get extra horse-power for driving the yacht forward.

There are various designs of staysail, and different ways of setting them. A good technique is to secure the sail to the windward toerail rather than a centre-line eye plate or cleat, so that it has a better chance of grabbing a big volume of wind.

A snap shackle or other quick-release device is needed at the tack, as well as at the halyard, because, like the spinnaker, this sail has to be handled quickly when racing. The sail is set flying, that is no hanks are secured to a stay, and the sail does not go up a luff groove. This means that when getting it in, good crew work is essential to prevent the sail billowing overboard.

Spinnaker staysail set on inner forestay

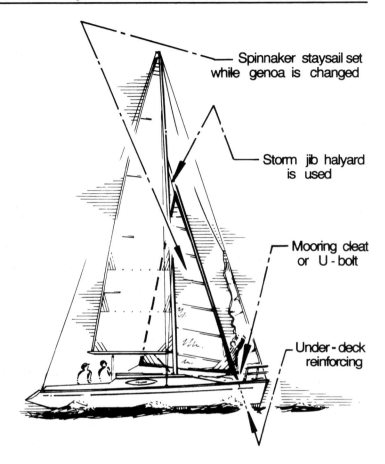

Spinnaker staysail set while genoa is changed

Storm jib halyard is used

Mooring cleat or U - bolt

Under - deck reinforcing

The spinnaker staysail shown here is the old-fashioned type, set on an inner forestay. However, some versions extend to near the masthead and are much narrower in proportion. A droop along the foot, not shown in the drawing, helps to improve efficiency because air flow cannot escape under the bottom of the sail.

This sail is handy for keeping a boat moving when the genoa has to be changed if there is a single-groove headsail foil or a single outer forestay. With twin grooves or twin forestays, the second genoa can be set before the other is taken in.

Instead of having the yacht 'bare-headed', with nothing working forward of the mast, this sail is set before lowering the genoa.

It is normally a fine weather sail of light cloth, but it can be made of heavy cloth, for rough weather.

It will cost more if made of strong sailcloth, but it will last longer and have more uses. For instance, it can be used downwind with a reefed mainsail in strong conditions when the crew cannot manage a spinnaker.

Using the windward sheet

Because the clew of a working jib is roughly in line with the mast, a pull on the windward sheet brings the clew inboard, as shown in this plan view. To get the sail flattened well inboard, it will almost certainly be necessary to slacken off the lee sheet slightly.

This operation slows the boat, but makes her point closer to the wind. Carried to the extreme, the clew ends up to windward of the mast, and the yacht is hoveto. She now 'fore-reaches', plugging gently to windward at a slow speed, with the mainsheet slackened off and the tiller pushed to leeward.

This is a good way to ride out rough weather, though it may not be safe in the worst conditions. The course is likely to have a big leeway component, so the true direction 'over the ground' may be to leeward, or across the wind.

Heaving-to like this is a great way to steady the yacht down for a period of relative peace in tough conditions. This can be useful for getting some sleep, cooking a meal, tucking a reef, getting ground tackle ready for entering harbour and so on.

On some yachts the sheet leads are poorly positioned, being too far outboard for going to windward. It is usual to rig Barber haulers to pull the sheet inwards under these circumstances, but sometimes this trick of tightening in the windward sheet can be used instead.

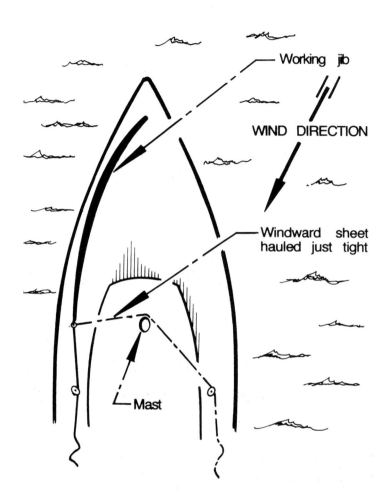

Working jib

WIND DIRECTION

Windward sheet hauled just tight

Mast

Headsail with built-in bag

By the time the working jib is being set, the wind is usually fresh, if not downright strong. The crew working on the foredeck want things kept as simple as possible, especially when far offshore in steep seas. Getting a sail out of its bag and hanked on to the forestay, or slid up the luff groove, can be a tricky business. Every year a thousand sail-bags are lost overboard in these conditions, quite apart from the other problems. For instance, if the sail has been badly stowed it will come out of the bag the wrong way.

Here is a new approach to the job of setting and taking in a working jib. The sail is made with its own integral bag, by stitching on an extra layer of cloth along the bottom. The top of the sail is stowed by folding it down and tucking it into the bag. The top of the bag coincides with the bottom seam. The tapes along the top of the bag are secured, once the sail has been packed away. The drawing shows the sail packed in its bag.

When setting the sail, the tack and sheets can be secured while the sail is still in its bag. The sail can be left on the foredeck, all ready for hanking on when

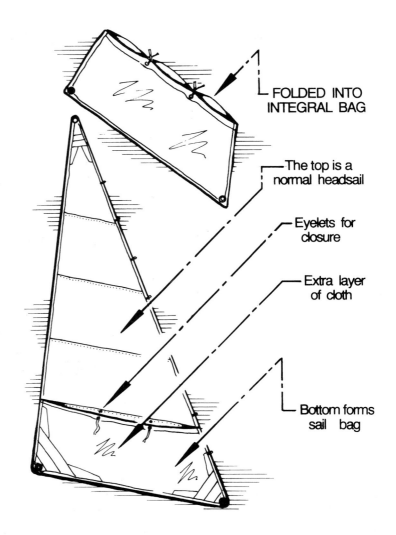

FOLDED INTO INTEGRAL BAG

The top is a normal headsail

Eyelets for closure

Extra layer of cloth

Bottom forms sail bag

conditions demand that the genoa is lowered and the working jib set.

One disadvantage of this idea is that the sail may get dirty. This can partly be overcome by using tanned Terylene or Dacron, because this does not show the dirt much. The line of the top of the bag can coincide with a reef, and the ties that secure the bag can act as reef points as well.

Folding an awkward sail

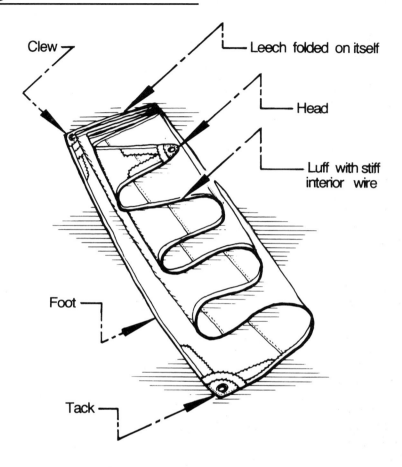

Clew

Leech folded on itself

Head

Luff with stiff interior wire

Foot

Tack

Some sails can be hard to fold because they have extra-stiff luffs. For instance, headsails with thick wire luff ropes, and extra-stout trisails, can be the very devil to pack up neatly.

Often the secret is to zig-zag fold the sail in the usual way, but to ensure the leech is folded over itself, as shown in the drawing. In practice it may be best to have the leech work inwards or outwards slightly, so that the edges of each fold are not precisely over the previous fold.

The aim is to have large curves along the stiff luff, so that the sail lies naturally and does not have to be forced into position. Luff wires must never be kinked or bent out of shape, so the head of the sail may end up beyond the leech, and not neatly on top of the last fold, as shown here.

There is no doubt that a sail of this type needs a large bag. It may help to turn to Chapter 8 on sail covers and bags to see how to make an existing bag larger without much cost.

4. Spinnakers

Light-wind spinnaker

A fault with spinnakers in gentle winds is their tendency to 'pleat' in the middle at the top. The lack of wind pressure results in a sail that does not spread out to its full width, so that one or more folds appear, extending down from near the spinnaker top. The stiffening at the head reduces this problem, but does not eliminate it.

Provided the class rules allow it, a spinnaker can be modified fairly easily by adding to the area of the stiffening at the head, so that in effect there is a wide headboard. However, this process needs careful workmanship and thoughtful design.

For a start, the sail must still be capable of being stowed. So if the boat has a spinnaker chute (as found on dinghies and some small racing classes), this technique will seldom be found to be practicable except in a limited way. It is a weakness of chutes that they do not hold spinnakers safely in rough weather unless the sail is totally inside.

Assuming the sail is set from one of the standard designs of 'turtle' or other type of special spinnaker bag, the top of the sail can be thickened so that it is

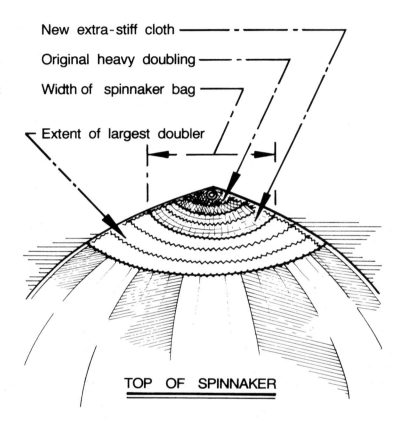

New extra-stiff cloth

Original heavy doubling

Width of spinnaker bag

Extent of largest doubler

TOP OF SPINNAKER

like thin plywood for the width of the bag opening. Normally the sailmaker will stitch on extra layers of a semi-stiff material or stout cloth. However, repeated rows of zig-zag stitching will give a comparable, though less effective, result.

Extending wider and lower than this serious additional stiffening, there can be a larger area that is less rigid. This part of the sail must be stiff enough to stay widespread in all breezes, but not so plank-like that it will not curl over to fit in the sailbag.

Low-cost spinnaker gear

The cost of the gear over and above the cost of the sail makes owners of cruisers hesitate before buying a spinnaker. However, there are cheap ways of getting 'up and running (downwind)'.

Inexpensive spinnaker booms are sometimes to be found. For instance, when a pole breaks it may be cheaper for an insurance company to provide a new one. Anyone good with tools can mend the damaged one, especially if it was originally longer than is now needed. Then there are those old wooden spinnaker booms that have been discarded in favour of the more modern aluminium ones. If all else fails, an alloy scaffold pole can often be made into an acceptable boom.

The fitting on the mast may be a single strong ring of the correct size to take the boom end fittings. In time, more rings can be riveted on, or the original fitting removed and a more normal arrangement of track and sliding eye put on the mast.

For a limited time, a spare jib halyard can be used for the spinnaker, but soon an extra block on a wire span to keep it forward and clear of

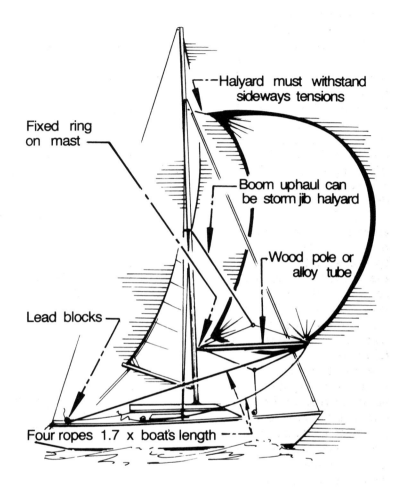

Fixed ring on mast

Halyard must withstand sideways tensions

Boom uphaul can be storm jib halyard

Wood pole or alloy tube

Lead blocks

Four ropes 1.7 x boat's length

obstructions will be needed, with a dedicated halyard.

The sheets, guys and halyard can be secondhand rope, provided it is in good order, because at this level of racing nothing is going to be massively stressed. None of the blocks need to be

precisely the correct size and type, especially as oversize blocks reduce friction and provide an extra safety factor. Under-size blocks should never be used.

And, of course, gear can be bought from a Boat Jumble.

Safe spinnaker setting – first stage

A good way to be sure that the spinnaker goes up swiftly and correctly is to have two or more of the crew check each item of gear. This drawing shows the sailbag secured on the port guard rail wires, ready for hoisting. It must be packed with no twists in it.

It is seldom necessary for a second person to go forward to ensure everything is led clear of obstructions, as most things can be seen from the cockpit. The sheets and guys must be clear outside the guard rails and over the top of them. The guy has to be in the pole end without a twist, and the pole has to be at the correct height.

On some yachts the boom uphaul rope has a mark on it, where it is jammed into its cleat. This means that the person raising the boom does not even have to look up when hoisting it, though a check should always be made to ensure the foredeck hand is out of the way.

A mark can also be made on the spinnaker halyard by its jam cleat, to ensure that it is neither too loose (and so liable to wrap itself round a cross tree), nor too tight (and so likely to drag the spinnaker out of the bag prematurely).

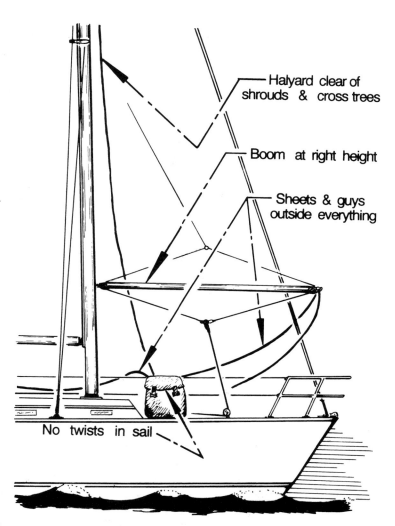

Halyard clear of shrouds & cross trees

Boom at right height

Sheets & guys outside everything

No twists in sail

This drawing accompanies the one opposite 'Safe spinnaker setting – second stage'.

If anyone in the crew is a beginner, it may help if both pictures are photocopied and stuck up at the fore end of the cockpit. The view shown is with the starboard guard-wires omitted for clarity.

Safe spinnaker setting – second stage

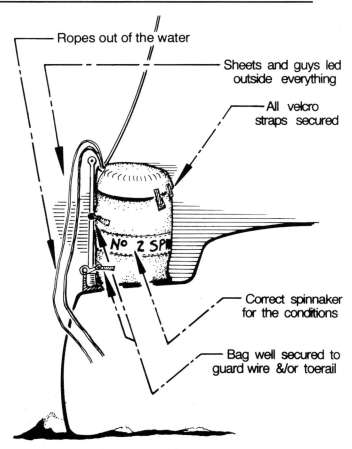

Ropes out of the water

Sheets and guys led
outside everything

All velcro
straps secured

No 2 SPI

Correct spinnaker
for the conditions

Bag well secured to
guard wire &/or toerail

Seen from aft, a spinnaker bag that has been set up inside the port guard rail wires should look like this. The crew in the cockpit can see the name on the bag, and this confirms they have the right kite for the prevailing weather. The bottom and middle of the bag are secured low down, so that when the halyard pulls the sail aloft, the bag stays put, the right way up.

All sheets and guys must extend out of the bag and up over the top wire, running forward or aft, outside the rails and clear of obstructions. They must be kept just tight enough to avoid dragging in the water. All the velcro straps that keep the top of the bag closed need to be secured down tightly, except perhaps in light airs when some of them may be left undone.

The halyard is often pulled down and a metre or two above the snap shackle stuffed down the side of the bag. Then if the wind catches the rope, instead of the sail being tugged out of the bag, the halyard just angles off to leeward in an arc. This has to be watched when rounding a mark closely, otherwise the rope may touch the mark.

Curing a twist

When hoisting a spinnaker, the crew watch anxiously to see if it has a twist in it as it starts to fill. A single turn in the sail often unwinds as the force of the wind stretches and spreads the sail. A more serious snarl-up may refuse to self-straighten, especially if the sail is wet.

It seldom pays to tweak or jolt the bottom of the sail, unless it is quite small and the crew can reach a substantial way up the leech. Likewise, jerking the sheet and guy, or slacking off the halyard, seldom works. There is one reliable cure..... often the quickest even with a small spin-naker..... drop the sail till the twist is within reach of the deck. The sail can then be manhandled, working the leeches apart.

If the twist looks small, the leeches can be pulled apart from the bottom, so that the top of the sail rotates. Even if there is no swivel on the halyard, it will rotate and take the snarls out of the sail without difficulty.

A very bad set of turns may have to be unfankled downwards, and the sheet freed to get the lee clew taken round and round the sail. If the sail suddenly fills when the sheet is not

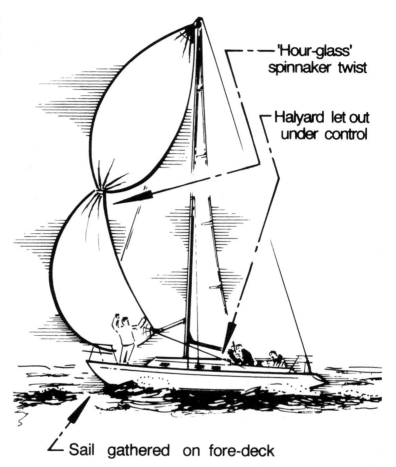

'Hour-glass' spinnaker twist

Halyard let out under control

Sail gathered on fore-deck

clipped on, the spinnaker may get out of control. To avoid this, the job is done in the lee of the mainsail and with more than one person on the job.

Experienced crews seem to have a magic ability that cures the trouble in sec-onds. Beginners could do worse than practise in fine weather, after deliberately hoisting the sail with a twist in it.

Gear for a shy spinnaker

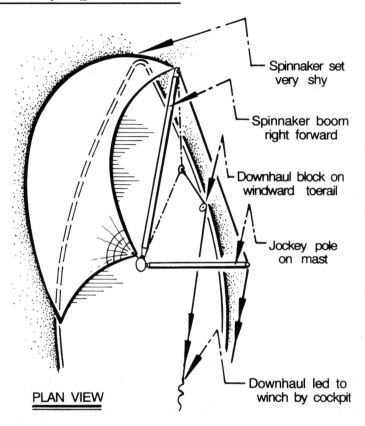

Spinnaker set very shy

Spinnaker boom right forward

Downhaul block on windward toerail

Jockey pole on mast

Downhaul led to winch by cockpit

PLAN VIEW

On small boats, the spinnaker gear seldom needs changing or modifying to suit different conditions. On a large yacht, if the spinnaker has to be set with a fierce wind on or forward of the beam, it pays to alter things.

For a start, the spinnaker boom should not be against the forestay. However, the pull of the guy is too nearly parallel with the boom, so getting the latter to swing away from the forestay can

be almost impossible. A jockey pole or bearing-out spar, secured at its inner end to the mast, transforms the situation because it angles the guy out to windward. This gives the crew that extra leverage needed to haul the boom back a fraction.

It is normal to have the spinnaker boom downhaul block in the middle of the deck; but for shy reaching, a block out on the windward toerail reduces the loads

and makes it easier to control the boom. The downhaul will need taking to a winch on all but the smallest yachts, once the loadings start to increase in concert with the wind strength.

Finally, the halyard should be tight up, even though this causes the main to blanket part of the spinnaker. In strong winds, control of the sail and yacht is more important than getting the last bit of high-speed air into the spinnaker.

Tell-tales on the spinnaker boom

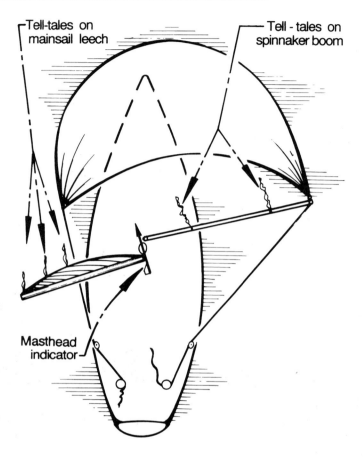

Tell-tales on
mainsail leech

Tell - tales on
spinnaker boom

Masthead
indicator

It is usual to have tell-tales on the luffs of sails, and on the leech of the mainsail. However, these tell-tales are not easy to watch when running, nor do they always warn the crew of subtle wind changes. Watching the masthead indicator can be hard work, as the neck has to be bent back a long way. On a big yacht, the 'hawk' at the top of the mast is so far away that it may be largely ineffective; quite apart from the fact that the wind direction at the masthead may be different from lower down.

For all these and other reasons, tell-tales on the spinnaker boom are worth considering. This boom is normally trimmed at right angles to the wind, so these tell-tales will give an early warning that the boom needs shifting. Like so many other things on a yacht, they have to be used in conjunction with other gear, and not treated as the only thing that matters.

Thin strips of nylon spinnaker cloth cut with a hot-knife make good tell-tales. They are glued to the boom, on the top or bottom, so that they blow clear on either gybe.

Avoiding spinnaker rips

In the course of a busy season a spinnaker may get a dozen tears, and sometimes three times that number. Even if the tears are tiny, they cannot be left unmended in case they spread; therefore the sail has to be taken to a sailmaker for repairs after each accident.

Some of these rips are hard to explain, others are the result of the sail slithering over the bow navigation light, or a deck fitting that has a slight protuberance. Careful crews will always tape over everything suspect.

A typical bow navigation light will have corners, sometimes fastenings that are not flush, and maybe a support plate with sharp edges, all of which can start a tear. The lifeline ends are notorious rip-starters, what with small angular shackles, wired-up rigging screws, split pins in clevis pins, and sometimes protruding strands at the ends of guard rail wires.

It is not enough to put tape on at the beginning of the season and forget it. Sunlight and weathering cause the tape to harden and start to peel off, so monthly checks and repairs are needed.

On yachts with chutes for

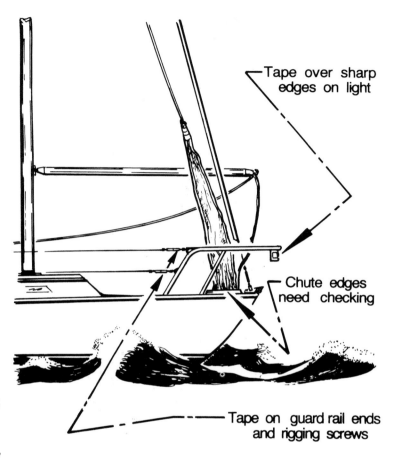

Tape over sharp edges on light

Chute edges need checking

Tape on guard rail ends and rigging screws

launching the spinnaker, it is extra important to ensure the exit of the 'tunnel' is totally smooth and well rounded. As it goes in or out of the chute, the spinnaker is under tension, so it must be given an easy passage. The use of fine sandpaper on the chute edges helps.

Helpful spinnaker colours

When packing a spinnaker in a hurry it is a help if the top of the sail is easily found due to it being a different colour from the rest of the sail. This is especially true if the work is being done in a dim cabin, perhaps at night with the help of a single fading light. If the two clews are also easy to find because the surrounding cloth is another distinctive colour, so much the better.

This suggests that the sail should be in three colours: one at the top; one covering much (if not all) of the middle; and one at the bottom. In practice, sailmakers tend to favour three roughly equal areas of colour, largely because this fits in the cloth lay-out that is most often used.

For cunning owners who race offshore, and do not want to be spotted from afar by the opposition, a top made of pale-blue cloth may help to emulate warships in the days of sail. In those times, the ability to sneak away unseen could be a matter of life and death, so all sorts of tricks were used, including taking in the higher sails when another vessel was in sight from the masthead. These days, with a pale-blue sky-coloured top, and perhaps a medium-

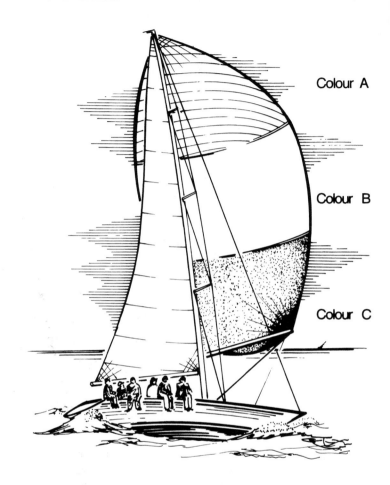

Colour A

Colour B

Colour C

blue middle designed to match the ocean's colour, one might gain miles before unobservant crews on other yachts realised what was happening.

Most spinnakers have distinctive corner patches, but these tend to get lost in the voluminous folds when the sail is in a muddle on the cabin sole. If more than one person is putting the spinnaker back in its bag, it is a help if the sail has these different colour bands because one person can work round the whole edge, taking out twists, while the second segregates the top and bottom in separate piles.

Safer spinnaker setting

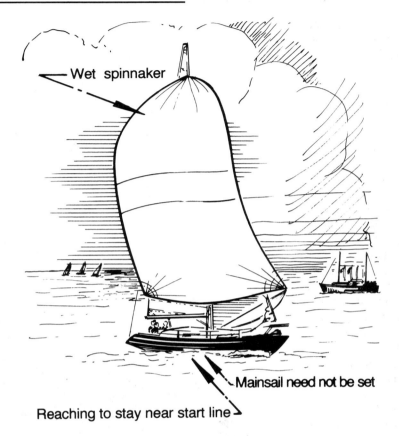

Wet spinnaker

Mainsail need not be set

Reaching to stay near start line

A wet spinnaker is harder to pack than a dry one. It is liable to stay twisted when hoisted, instead of burgeoning and starting to pull without delay. If it goes up with a twist and it is saturated, it can be a real fight to sort out the fankle.

However, there is often time before a race starts to fly the spinnaker for at least a few minutes, to reduce the amount of water it has blotted up. Assuming the wind is light or moderate, the best technique is to reach back and forth, because this means the yacht does not get too far from the start line. Just as important, there is plenty of drying wind surging across the front and back of the sail.

Even if the sail cannot be set for more than a brief period, this will have a useful effect. A spinnaker gets progressively easier to handle as the water trapped in the folds and the cloth is reduced. If there is no time or opportunity to hoist the sail, it can be bundled loosely on deck, and perhaps draped over the guard rails to dry it.

When it comes to dropping the spinnaker after a drying session, the yacht should be run off dead downwind to reduce the chances of the sail going into the water and getting wet again.

In control downwind

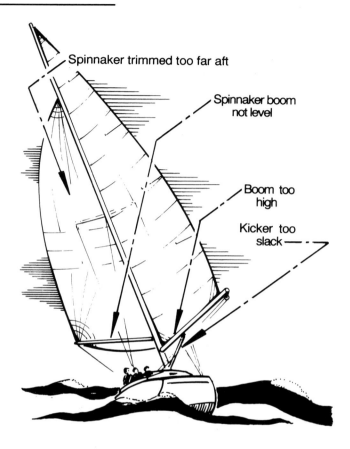

Spinnaker trimmed too far aft

Spinnaker boom
not level

Boom too
high

Kicker too
slack

To prevent rolling and broaching under spinnaker, a few simple rules should be followed. The spinnaker has to be well forward so the sheet and guy need easing. Both ropes should be led down to the deck much further forward than usual. This may be done by shifting the blocks or by having separate controls (which are sometimes called 'twing lines') to haul the ropes down to deck level roughly amidships.

The spinnaker halyard must be tight up, as must the kicker or vang. Tightening the kicker is usually impossible with roller reefing once the main is rolled down, which is one reason why this form of reefing has fallen from favour. On keenly-sailed racing yachts, the kicker control is led to both the port and starboard sides so that it can either be controlled by two people, or can be worked from the most convenient side.

The mainsheet must be well off, and sometimes the main is reefed before the smaller spinnaker is set, assuming the yacht carries both a normal and a heavy weather spinnaker. The ability to reef while running before a hard breeze is a great asset, and this is a sail change that is well worth practising.

Heavy weather gybe

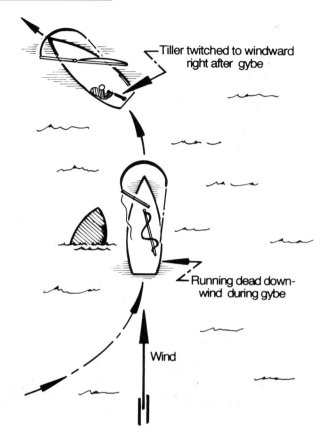

Tiller twitched to windward right after gybe

Running dead down-wind during gybe

Wind

A gybe in blustery conditions is a team effort. The foredeck crew and the helmsman have to work together and the rest of the crew follow their lead. The actual gybe is done when running dead downwind, even if the course is from reach to reach.

The hand on the mainsail has to ensure that the sheet is let off fast, with lots of slack, so that there is no tendency for the mainsail to cause a broach as it fills on the new lee side. An extra pair of hands may be needed here to ensure the rope runs out quickly and smoothly.

The helmsman warns the foredeck as he brings the course straight downwind and holds the course steady in spite of the boisterous conditions. Quick handling of the spinnaker boom ensures there is no time for the spinny to take charge and, to this end, the eye or socket on the mast has to be down where it can be reached easily.

As the spinnaker fills on the new gybe, the helmsman briefly brings the helm to windward to prevent the yacht surging up into a windward broach. The sheet handlers do not tighten in too quickly until the crew weight is to windward and everyone on board is alert to the possibility of a broach.

Easier spinnaker handling

Even experienced crews get worried when it comes to gybing the spinnaker boom in wild conditions. The main problem is getting the inboard end of the boom hooked into its eye on the front of the mast. The following simple idea can make all the difference.

A length of rope has a loop knotted in one end, and this loop is passed up through the spinnaker's eye on the front of the mast before the gybe. As soon as the spinnaker boom end is inboard and ready for clipping on, the loop is clipped into the boom end, so the situation is as shown in the drawing.

One of the crew, aft of the mast, pulls on the rope, using a winch if need be. This forces the inboard end of the boom right on to the eye. The foredeck hand opens the plunger, so that the rope loop comes off, and the boom is clipped in place at the same time. Like all sail handling techniques, this trick needs practice.

If the loop jams in place when the boom is clipped on, the rope is cut and a new loop made. The rope should be as light as possible so that it renders round the eye easily. One improvement is a turning block down near the deck, below

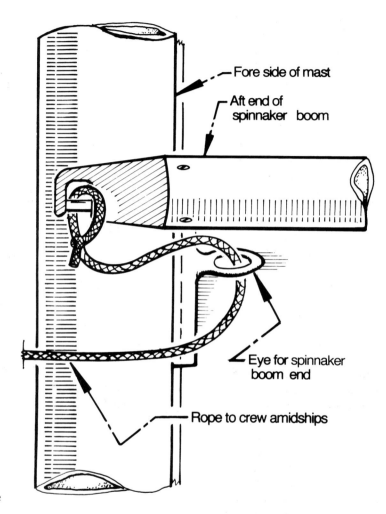

Fore side of mast

Aft end of spinnaker boom

Eye for spinnaker boom end

Rope to crew amidships

the eye, to lead the rope aft. This will ease the work on the rope and avoid a sharp turn of the rope at the eye.

Whatever size of rope is used, it should be thick enough to give a good grip, so anything under ⅜ in (10 mm) is almost bound to be too thin.

One experienced foredeck hand has described this as the best idea since the invention of the spinnaker. Another has said that it is a complete waste of time and no substitute for skill!

Spinnaker release hook

Snap shackles can be the very devil to release. When under load, even the best type sometimes require a very strong jerk to get the pivoted end to burst open. It is usual to have a small rope loop through the metal eye on the end of the plunger, but even that does not always give an adequate grip for opening the snap shackle.

A special hook for doing the job is a tremendous help, especially on large yachts. The hook may be made of ⁵/₁₆ or ³/₈ in (8 or even 10 mm) steel with a rounded end so that it does not tear the spinnaker by accident. The length of the hook will vary to suit different yachts and foredeck hands, and it will also depend on whether the crew are standing on the foredeck or working in a bosun's chair above deck. An over-all length of about 10 in (25 cm) suits many situations, but some people will prefer 50 per cent longer, while others favour 50 per cent shorter.

Everyone agrees that the handle has to be a comfortable fit, and so of the order of 4 in (10 cm) across, or 7 in (18 cm) for two-handed operations. The diameter will be about

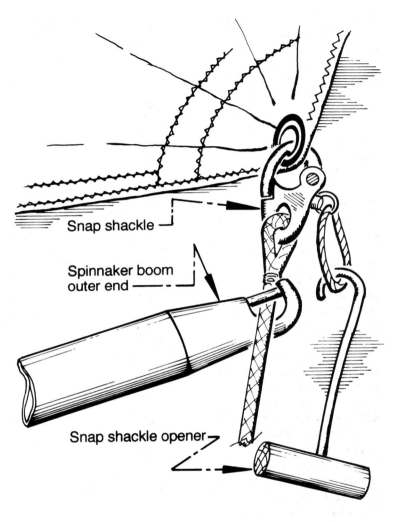

Snap shackle

Spinnaker boom outer end

Snap shackle opener

1¼ in (3 cm) in order to give a strong grip.

A safety line on the hook is essential, and most yachts will require at least one spare hook..... more will be lost overboard than will wear out!

Spinnaker tamer

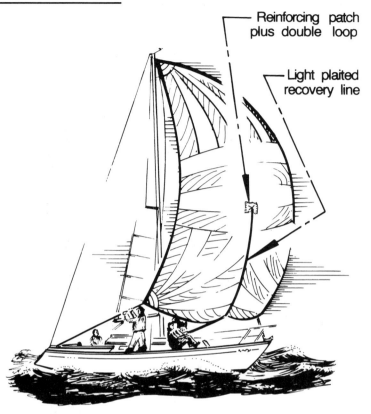

Reinforcing patch
plus double loop

Light plaited
recovery line

Getting a spinnaker down is usually easy enough even in strong winds, provided the sail is hauled in under the lee of the mainsail. Admittedly some people have trouble gripping the flapping nylon, and others are not quick enough in smothering the voluminous folds of cloth.

What can be a great help is a recovery line. This is a light plaited rope made fast to two strong tape loops stitched to the middle of the spinnaker. A reinforcing patch of double or treble thickness, well spread over the sail, is needed to take the loops and contain the loads. This patch will be on both sides of the sail.

The beauty of this idea is that it can be used on a new or old sail. It can be used on all sizes of spinnaker, and on larger ones two recovery lines can be fitted at different heights. The idea can be adapted for asymmetrical spinnakers and for all sorts of cruising chutes, mizzen staysails; in fact any sail that is set flying and inclined to sag off to leeward when being taken in.

Ideally, the recovery line should be on the fore side of the sail, so that it folds the sail in half and spills the wind out both sides. But the line works almost as well if it is on the aft or windward side of the sail.

Dealing with a ripping spinnaker

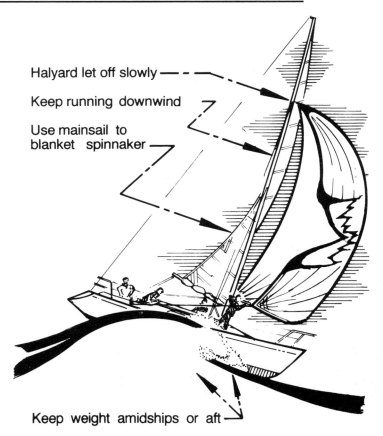

Halyard let off slowly

Keep running downwind

Use mainsail to blanket spinnaker

Keep weight amidships or aft

It is so tempting to rush forward when a spinnaker tears dramatically. Certainly speed is needed to limit the area of damage and get the sail quickly stowed below. But in heavy winds it is important on many yachts to keep weight off the bow to prevent broaching. So some thought as well as action is needed.

A recognised technique is to gather the torn sail under the main boom, keeping it shielded behind the mainsail so that it does not thrash about much. The guy has to be let go and the sheet taken in, but both jobs need doing with care.

One person kneeling on the lee sidedeck can take in the sail and hold it down on a small or medium-size yacht. Larger yachts need a complete team. Every yacht needs someone in charge of the operation to ensure that the halyard is let off smoothly, and not so fast that the head of the torn sail bellies forward and starts going berserk. It is often best to let the helmsman concentrate on steering while the spinnaker trimmer copes with the crises.

As soon as possible a start should be made on drying the spinnaker, because it is hard to make a good job of the repair if water is running off the cloth on to the sewing machine!

5. Storm Jibs and Trisails

Storm jib improvements

If the corners of the storm jib are coloured, and made of different material, they can be recognised easily as they come out of the sail-bag. Also, a splash of bright orange at the head of the sail makes the yacht easier to see when the ocean is covered in driven spume. All the corner doublings on this sail should be larger than on working jibs.

That bright orange PVC cloth used for covers on RNLI lifeboats makes a tough outer layer for the top corner, and its smooth feel is easy to recognise in the dark. The bottom corner might be tanned Terylene of the heaviest weave.

It is a great advantage if the headsail hanks can be clipped on with one hand, and the 'dog's lead' type fulfil this specification. They also tend to have a bigger jaw opening than other types, which further helps when battling on the fore-deck in rough conditions.

In the very worst weather the hanks take a lot of pun-ishment and tend to break or tear off, so it makes sense to have them closely spaced. Then if one fails, the adjacent hanks are not grossly overloaded.

If conditions go from terrible to frantic, it is a help if the storm jib can be reduced in area to a 'hand-kerchief' by reefing it down. The reef eyes need to be as big as the chunky corner eyes and the reef points close-spaced..... also very strong.

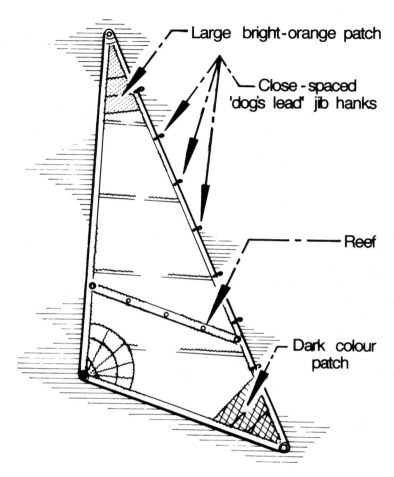

Large bright-orange patch

Close-spaced 'dog's lead' jib hanks

Reef

Dark colour patch

Tack pennant on a storm jib

It is quite common to find that the sheet lead tracks do not extend far enough forward to give a proper lead for storm jib sheets. This problem is overcome by having a tack pennant, so that the whole sail sets further up the forestay.

There are plenty of subsidiary advantages to this arrangement. The crew have a better view under the sail, even when the yacht heels a lot in strong winds. Also, by having the whole sail above the lifelines, chafe is reduced.

The pennant has traditionally been made of flexible wire rope, usually spliced directly into the tack eye on the sail. The bottom end has a hard eye and a large strong snap shackle which is easy to clip on to the deck fitting. Anyone who cannot splice wire can use Terylene/Dacron rope, which is so easy to splice. It is important to select strong rope that can stand up to the worst weather. To be doubly safe, it should be 50 per cent stronger than the halyard.

This trick of raising the whole sail up the forestay can be used whenever the sheet lead track does not extend sufficiently far forward, provided the headsail

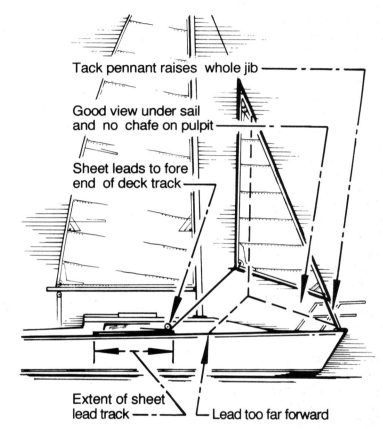

Tack pennant raises whole jib

Good view under sail and no chafe on pulpit

Sheet leads to fore end of deck track

Extent of sheet lead track

Lead too far forward

is one that does not have a luff as long as the forestay, so that it can be hoisted well above the deck.

Sometimes it can be cheaper and quicker to re-cut a sail instead of moving the sheet lead track, or fitting an extension piece at the fore end to lengthen the track, especially as there are two tracks: one port, one starboard.

Storm jib details

Properly-made storm jibs are triple stitched..... all the seams are joined by three rows of zig-zag stitching. On yachts over about 43 ft (13 m) it is becoming common for this sail to have quadruple stitching: four rows of strong zig-zagging to stand up to chafe in the wildest sea conditions.

Naturally the edges have extra stitching too, and the patches at the corners are massively thick, again with more than the usual runs of stitching. The eyes for the hanks have to be extra strong and are usually of the same type as those used at the corners of the sails. They have a stainless steel inner rim and are cramped in place by a hydraulic press. The cheap light brass eyes that are hammered in place are often found to be inadequate in storm winds.

The corner eyes should be extra large for strength, but in practice some sailmakers fit eyes that accord with the *size* of the sail, and they ignore its use. This can mean that the yacht's normal jib sheets will not both fit through the clew eye. This drawing shows the answer to the problem: one sheet is knotted through and the second one is knotted into the loop made by the first bowline.

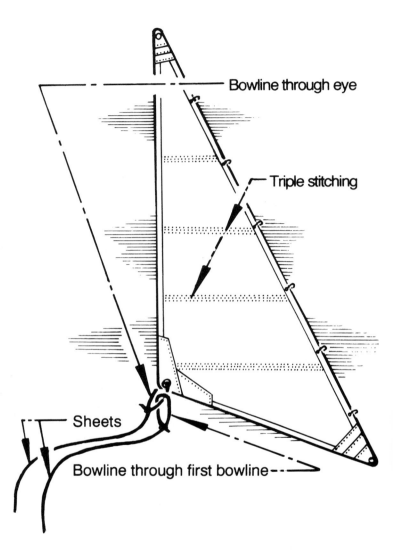

Bowline through eye

Triple stitching

Sheets

Bowline through first bowline

Storm jibs are seldom used, and so when they are needed in 'battle conditions' there may be some unexpected snag, such as the two sheets not fitting through the clew eye. It is a sensible idea to try out storm sails in moderate conditions, to make sure there are no hidden problems.

Storm-proof sails

There is a lot of difference between a bad autumn gale and a real storm. The latter can be so severe that after sailing through it, both the trisail and storm jib may have taken such a battering that they need massive repairs or even replacing.

Things that seem normal and acceptable on sails, like plastic luff slides, will not stand up to the terrible thrashing of a real storm. It is essential to have metal luff slides, and they should be kept lightly greased so they slide up the track without demanding too much sweating on the halyard..... the crew will almost certainly be tired when setting this sail. Besides, the yacht will be hurled about so much by the seas that she will not be a good platform for sail handling.

The same considerations apply to jib hanks. They must be close together to stand up to the tremendous strains. It is quite usual for the top and bottom ones to come adrift, so the next in line need to be nearby. These hanks should be at least one size up, compared to those on the other sails on board. They, too, need lightly greasing, otherwise they may be found to be seized when wanted. Stainless steel rather than

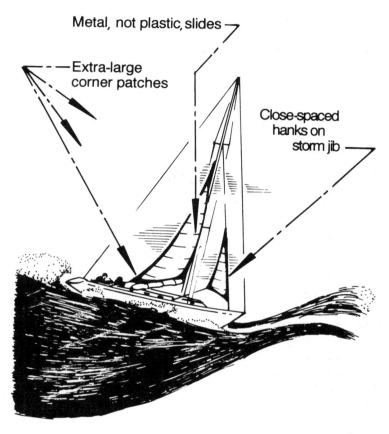

Metal, not plastic, slides

Extra-large corner patches

Close-spaced hanks on storm jib

bronze hanks are best as they tend to be tougher, wear better and are less likely to seize.

The corners of storm sails need to be extensive and much thicker than on other sails. If the clew of the storm jib touches the shrouds, and the boat has

to tack in severe conditions, the outer cloths may be shredded quickly by the vicious impact. *Small* hydraulically-pressed eyes cannot stand this sort of punishment, and the old-fashioned hand-worked eyes lose their over-sewn threads in seconds.

Trisail shape and size

The top of a trisail should not go above the crosstrees, so that if the top of the mast breaks off, this sail can be set from a block lashed to the top of the stump. Even if the mast does not break, the main halyard may fail totally, so that an emergency halyard block secured at the crosstrees has to be used. On masts with two or more sets of crosstrees, the top of the trisail is designed to terminate just below whichever set of crosstrees seems to make most sense.

The tack should be just above the stowed mainsail, or not far below the top of this sail when it is bunched on the boom. Different tack arrangements are used, including a line from the tack eye taken round the gooseneck and knotted there.

The clew may be positioned so that separate port and starboard sheets lead back to blocks on the toe rails or on eye plates bolted well aft. Sometimes the clew is secured round the main boom with a lashing that goes right round the stowed mainsail, and then the mainsheet is used in the ordinary way.

When it comes to area, there are different views.

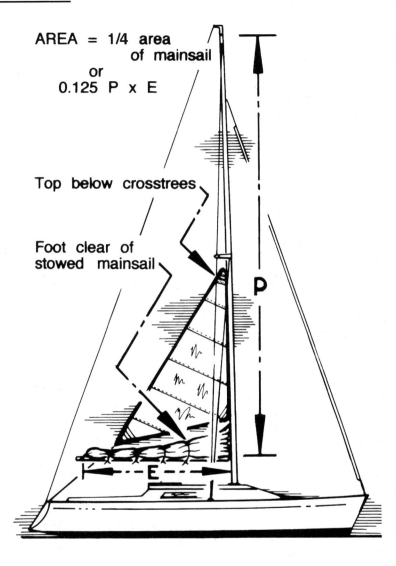

AREA = 1/4 area of mainsail
or
$0.125\ P \times E$

Top below crosstrees

Foot clear of stowed mainsail

P

E

The most common opinion is that the trisail should be one-quarter of the mainsail area, and this will do up to force 10 under most circumstances. Above this wind speed few sails will stand for long. Some owners like a larger trisail, with a reef for really worrying weather.

Using a jib as a trisail

In general, this idea only works if the jib is cut low so that the sheeting angle is right. Anyone buying a small headsail can have it designed to serve both as a heavy-duty working jib and as a trisail by ensuring that the angle at the clew suits both jobs.

Offshore cruisers and hard-up owners like this idea, since in effect they get two sails for the price of one plus the cost of a set of extra slides. These slides fit the track on the mast, and each one has a small strong loop on it, to which a jib hank is clipped. Naturally, there must be a few spare slides-with-loops on board in case some get lost.

Because this is a high-aspect sail, its performance to windward is good relative to its size. The tack can be set below the furled mainsail, as shown here, or even lower, partly closing the gap below the sail for added efficiency.

Some people prefer to have two sheets leading to the aft end of the deck rather than a single one to the boom end. The thinking here is that if the boom breaks, this sail deals with the crises. However, in heavy weather it is attractive to be able to put the helm over and have the

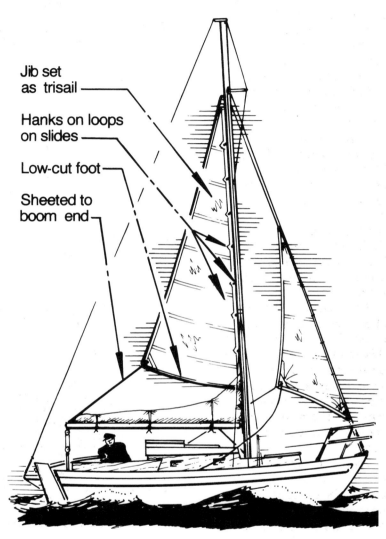

Jib set as trisail

Hanks on loops on slides

Low-cut foot

Sheeted to boom end

'tri-jib' tack itself because it is sheeted to the boom end. Also, when broad reaching or running free, the boom-end sheeting is far more effective. Either way, many

yachts will go to windward quite well under this sail alone, which adds to its other attractions.

6. Long-range Sailing and Offshore Cruising

Rig for long-range cruising

Plenty of people make extended cruises in yachts with semi-racing rigs designed for coastal cruising. Quite often these owners get away with the risks they are taking because they stay in relatively quiet, safe areas. However, the risks should be faced.

The traditional long-range rig consists of a low mast strongly supported by out-size rigging. Before changing all the standing rigging it is essential to ensure that the chain plates will take the next size up of toggle, because each item..... wire, rigging screw, toggle and chain plate..... has to fit its neighbour. Manufacturing tolerances are now tight and it is not always possible to select a heavier part and expect it to link on to adjacent components.

Rig stresses are kept as low as possible by fitting long, thick, tough cross-trees. Where jumper struts are fitted, they too should be much stouter than usual.

Moving parts like the gooseneck, genoa sheet leads, mainsheet parts, and so on, are all one or two sizes larger, thicker and stronger than those used for coastal cruising.

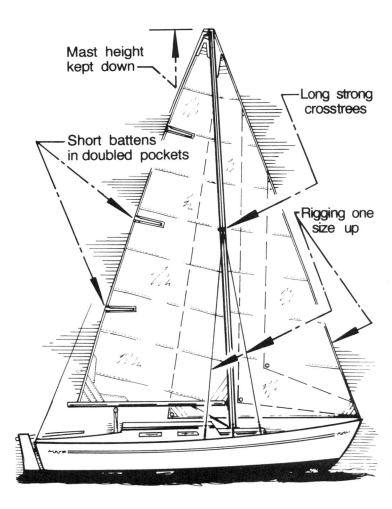

Mast height kept down

Long strong crosstrees

Short battens in doubled pockets

Rigging one size up

Battens and their pockets are often a source of trouble, but problems can be minimised by having three, instead of the more usual four, battens. If they are kept short with doubled or even trebled cloth forming the pockets, they should give long, reliable service. If they are made the same length, the spares position is easier.

Being seen at sea

Yachts are astonishingly hard to see at sea, in spite of their tall masts and broad spread of sails. Part of the problem is that the hull spends a lot of time hidden in troughs between waves, and these deep valleys can hide half the rig, even when the weather is not particularly rough.

To make matters worse, the sails may blend in with distant clouds and the seascape of breaking waves. There have been plenty of instances when an officer on watch on the bridge of a merchant ship has been unable to pick out a yacht less than half a mile away. This leads to accidents in which the yacht tends to come off worst.

Quite a small modification to a sail can make all the difference. If the top panel is made from high-visibility orange cloth, it will stand out like a flashing light. It is true that this type of sailcloth may have different characteristics to adjacent cloths, but for an offshore cruising sail these differences are normally acceptable. In fog, the 'shouting' colour is even more valuable, and may alert a ship on a collision course just in time.

Because no one can tell what sail will be set at any

Bright-orange top panels

date in the future, or what combination of sails, it is logical to have the top panel of most of the sails made ultra-easy to see. This coloured cloth has another advantage..... there is no problem finding the top of the sail when it is jumbled up in a sailbag.

Metal corners

The weakest places on most sails are the corners. It is therefore common sense to make them of metal, since this seldom wears to any measurable extent.

The head, tack and clew can all have either circular rings or D-shaped ones. Stainless steel is the preferred material, but in far-away places where this material is not available, clever sailors have been known to get a sheet of bronze, perhaps from a scrap heap, and cut out a metal shape to make a reliable corner. It is important to round off all edges to prevent chafing the sailcloth.

Standard sail-makers' rings are made from round section rod, bent to shape. The ends are welded together then the join is ground smooth. For the best appearance, the weld is hidden inside the corner of the sail.

Apart from doubler cloths folded over, which form the major securing arrangement of the corner, three or more tapes are sewn through the ring and well into the sail. These take the chafe on the sail and they last a long time because they are so tough. In time they will show signs of wear but they are easy to renew. Sometimes additional tapes

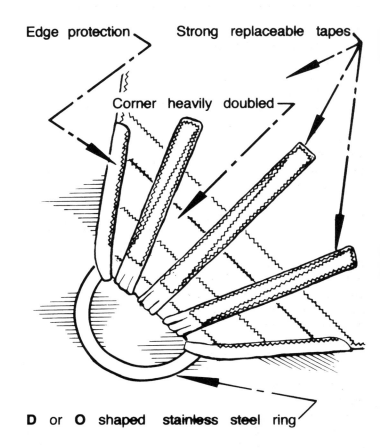

Edge protection

Strong replaceable tapes

Corner heavily doubled

D or O shaped stainless steel ring

are sewn on, leaving the original ones in place.

This type of corner has subsidiary advantages. At the clew there is usually more room for tying on large sheets as compared with a standard pressed-in corner eye. At the head it is seldom necessary to have a special 'long-legged' halyard shackle to reach into the sail to get to the pressed-in eye.

At the tack, a snap shackle with a fork end can

be secured easily to this type of corner. Some sail-makers use a snap shackle which has an integral eye on the end, and they make this eye the corner ring of the tack.

As with so many ideas in sail-making, the use of a metal ring may cost more at first, but it can save plenty of money in the long run. A ring will last forever so when the sail finally 'dies' the rings can be used on the replacement sail.

Offshore cruising mainsail

When a yacht leaves port on a long voyage, the things that normally wear first and wear worst on the sails must either be eliminated or made extra long-lasting.

Batten pockets are a constant source of worry, so many sailmakers recommend that they are left off. This results in a loss of sail area, because the leech must be cut slightly hollow. If the loss is unacceptable, the sail can sometimes be made longer at the foot so that it extends to near the end of the boom. Alternatively, the boom and the mainsail may both be made longer.

Chafing pieces are common at crosstree level, but they can be made more effective if they consist of multiple layers of cloth separately sewn. When the outer layer is worn, it can easily be cut off and the next layer exposed. There have to be sets of these protecting layers where the crosstrees chafe when the sail is fully hoisted and when it is reefed.

The reef eyes down the leech are made larger than usual, partly for extra strength and long life, but also to ensure that the reef lines run easily when being hauled down. If the luff reef eyes are tightened down by ropes, and not merely pulled down by hand and engaged on hooks at the fore end of the boom, then they too should be extra large.

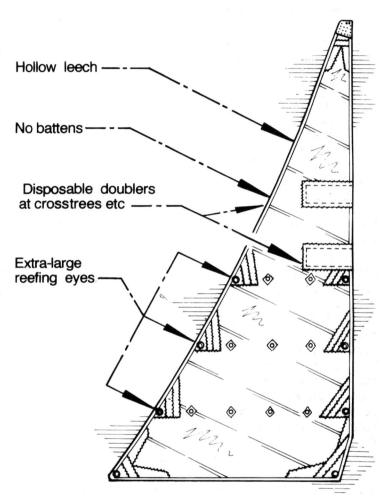

Hollow leech — · —

No battens — · —

Disposable doublers at crosstrees etc — · —

Extra-large reefing eyes

Offshore cruising headboard

If a sail has to last on a long voyage it needs to be extra tough and corrosion-proof. Alloy headboards and rivets suffer from corrosion after months of use, so the one shown here is made either of marine ply or a heavy gauge of inert plastic, or possibly even of bronze sheet metal, though this will almost certainly be costly.

Bronze fastenings last amazingly well, even when wet with salt water and baked by tropical sunshine. Whatever fastenings are used, there must be plenty of them, to spread all the loads and provide a factor of safety.

A weakness in many standard headboards is at the hole for the halyard shackle, so this one has a spare hole. Admittedly the lead of the halyard from the aft hole may be less than perfect, but at least if the forward hole becomes too oval, or wears badly, there is a back-up.

On any deep-water cruising mainsail the corner doublers are extra thick and extensive. Having the outer cloths at the head made of bright-orange cloth will improve the chances of the yacht being seen in rough weather. Even if the brightly coloured cloth only extends a couple of hand-spans

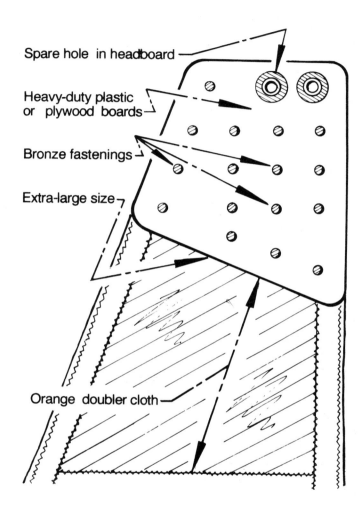

Spare hole in headboard

Heavy-duty plastic or plywood boards

Bronze fastenings

Extra-large size

Orange doubler cloth

down the sail, it is more likely to be seen than an all-white or care-worn grey sail.

Naturally, the further down the sail the orange colour extends the better, and a good case can be

made for having both top cloths in high-visibility orange. This also gives the yacht a distinctive appearance, which is recognisable at a much greater distance than numbers – even large ones.

Longer-lasting headsail

These ideas suit yachts used on long races or cruises, far from sailmakers who can carry out repairs. They add to the initial cost of a sail, but they tend to pay for themselves more than twice over in the long run.

Instead of the usual cheap 'hammered-in' eyelets for the luff hanks, choose the much stronger, longer-lasting, hydraulically pressed eyes. These are the same type of eye (but smaller in diameter) that is used for the tack, head and clew. To enhance them further, they have a broad strip of tough leather under the eye and round the luff to protect the sailcloth.

Where the sail touches stanchions and the pulpit, a piece of thick cloth is wrapped round the foot and zig-zag stitched. These doublers are rounded at the corners to eliminate another weak point, and there are at least two rows of stitching.

For the seams, edges, and so on, there is an extra row (or maybe even two extra rows) of stitching. Wear on stitching is almost always the first trouble that sails suffer from, so a back-up line of zig-zagging means there is strength and safety even after sub-stantial use.

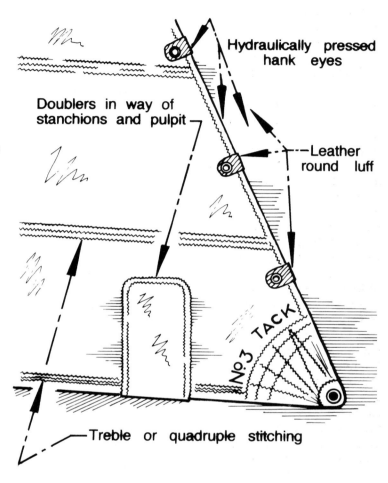

Doublers in way of stanchions and pulpit

Hydraulically pressed hank eyes

Leather round luff

No.3 TACK

Treble or quadruple stitching

These ideas can be worked into existing sails; and anyone setting off on a major voyage can often save money by having these additions put on to a good used sail to extend its life and make it as near failure-free as possible.

Offshore cruiser's light headsail

Long-range sailors try to avoid passages to windward. At worst, they like to close-reach, ideally in winds that are not too strong. Therefore they need a headsail that is cheap, reliable and easy to stow. A nylon No 1 genoa can be one of the handiest sails on board when a major offshore voyage is undertaken, and is often used on coastal cruisers.

Because the sail is made of nylon it is cheaper, and stows in a smaller space than a Terylene/Dacron one. It is no good when going to windward but, slightly off the wind, it comes into its own. It keeps even a heavy yacht going through light and fluky winds. In such conditions, the crew may take the mainsail down to save it from chafe, and because it slats back and forth in a maddening way. This is when the nylon headsail pays for itself.

It should be big to get the best from the fickle breeze, so it normally has a big overlap and a low foot. The crew need to be able to keep a good lookout all round, so the foot will not be extended right aft along the deck. To ensure that the yacht is easily seen in foggy or rain-ridden conditions, it makes sense to have the sail in a bright-red or other obtrusive colour. All sailmakers stock nylon in assorted colours because owners like cheerful spinnakers.

This sail is sometimes made to set 'flying' with no headsail hanks. This saves money but it can make the sail a handful to set and take in, especially if it has been carried too long in a rising breeze.

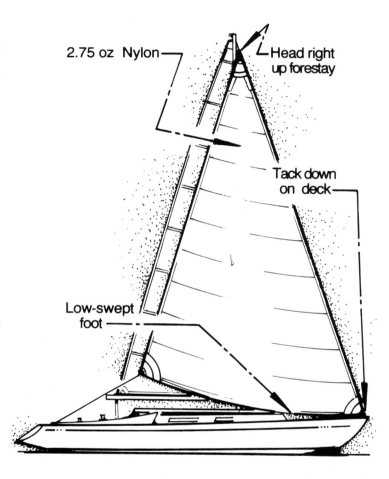

2.75 oz Nylon

Head right up forestay

Tack down on deck

Low-swept foot

Securing the mainsail

There's a popular idea that once the mainsail cover is fitted the mainsail is safe in all circumstances. This has never been true, and now that so many yachts are kept in marinas, the mainsail cover is even less reliable. When a yacht is on a swinging mooring, strong winds blow from ahead, and the mast partly protects the mainsail cover. In a marina, the wind comes from all directions, and the cover cannot be relied upon to stay in place and be so secure that it holds the mainsail safely.

To make matters worse, plenty of mainsail covers are made as cheaply as possible, with no reserve strength or extra securing arrangements. When a storm blasts over the yacht, the cover may fail within a few minutes, exposing the mainsail to the rough treatment of the shrieking wind. It is not unusual for a mainsail to be totally destroyed under these circumstances.

For safety there should be plenty of tiers round the mainsail, each one pulled tight but not enough to 'torture' the mainsail. As a rough guide, put a sail tier on at 'one arm's stretch' from the next; that is roughly 3 ft (1 m). They should be closer on boats under 30 ft (9 m). Double-knot each tier because if one fails, the wind will get under a fold of the sail and tease it free in an hour..... then the next tier will fail..... and so on.

It is especially important to lash the head of the sail well because if it thrashes back and forth it will disintegrate, in time, and repairs will be costly.

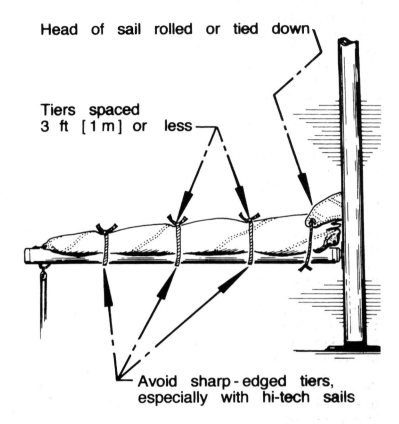

Head of sail rolled or tied down

Tiers spaced 3 ft [1 m] or less

Avoid sharp-edged tiers, especially with hi-tech sails

Heavy-duty tape

Some sailmakers use a handy strong tape for various jobs. It is about ½ in (12 mm) wide, double thickness, and soft to the touch. The tape is flexible and easy to thread through reef eyes on mainsails and mizzens, provided the eyelet holes are large enough, so it is ideal for bunching up the bunt of the sail once a reef has been hauled down.

Other sail tying materials tend to be too wide for use as reef points. Just as important, many of them have sharp edges that damage sails, especially those with thin film outer layers over strong internal threads.

This tape is also good for securing a headsail on the foredeck after a smaller one has been hauled up, as the weather gets tougher. It is never easy to fix a rope to any structure by putting a screw or bolt through it, whereas this tape holds fastenings well provided that round-headed ones are used and a large washer is put under the head in order to spread the load on the tape.

Using screws (or better still bolts), lengths of this tape can be secured to the deck or toe rail forward, for holding sails after they have been dropped. Because it ties easily, but is easy to untie, this tape is wonderful when hands are wet and cold.

Soft narrow sail tiers make good reef lines

Also good deck lashings

Clever stowage on deck

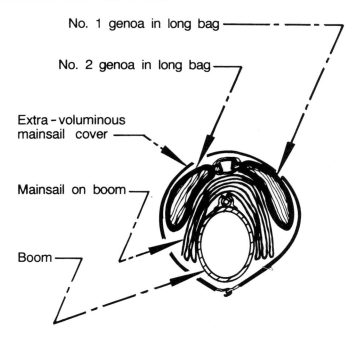

No. 1 genoa in long bag

No. 2 genoa in long bag

Extra - voluminous mainsail cover

Mainsail on boom

Boom

VIEW LOOKING FORWARD OR AFT

A shortage of sail stowage space is a common problem. It can be acute after a day's racing, when the crew want to go below to eat, drink and yarn, then get some sleep. The last thing they want is a cabin full of sails, especially wet ones.

The mainsail will be stowed on the boom in the usual way. There is no reason why headsails should not be folded into their long tubular bags and stowed beside the mainsail, as shown in the drawing.

These long bags have handles stitched beside the full-length zips, so the handles of two long bags can be lashed together using sail tiers. Then the headsails are laid along the length of the boom, on top of the folded mainsail, out of the way. Their weight holds them secure, like the panniers that hang each side of a pack-horse.

This technique requires an extra-large mainsail cover to fit over the two headsails in their bags, as well as the stowed mainsail. However, an existing normal mainsail cover can usually be enlarged to fit over the two extra sails.

It may be impossible to match the new cloth that forms the side extensions of the cover with the old cloth. In this situation it will be best to use a different-coloured cloth to give an attractive and distinctive sail cover that it easy to pick out from a distance. In a crowded mooring or marina, this is a help when looking for the yacht.

Folding a mainsail

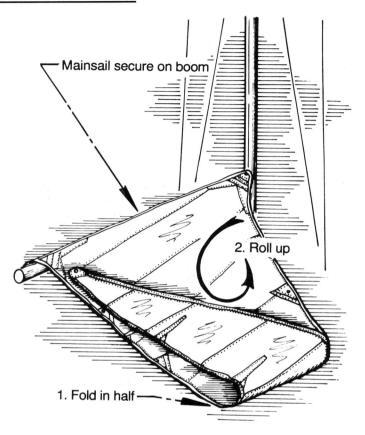

— Mainsail secure on boom

2. Roll up

1. Fold in half

Folding sails can be hard work, especially if there are only a few people available for the job. Many sails are better rolled than folded to preserve their racing efficiency, but it can be awkward rolling a sail from the head right to the foot.

One trick is to fold the sail in half, then roll it from the fold. To make this job easier (especially if it's breezy), the headboard can be lashed to the boom outer end with a sail tier. This keeps it in place till the sail has been rolled right up, and some tiers have been put round the middle of the sail and the boom. Then the head will probably have to be freed off before completing the stow and putting the sail cover on.

By tying the head to the outer end of the boom the leech is kept together, and the rolling should go well as the battens are normally at right angles to the leech. Even if, for one reason or another, the headboard cannot be tied to the aft end of the boom, this 'fold first, then roll' technique is a good one. In practice, quite a lot of people prefer to fold the head over less than halfway down..... some just fold in the top quarter or even the top eighth of the sail. The idea is still a good one, and speeds up stowing the mainsail.

Folding a headsail

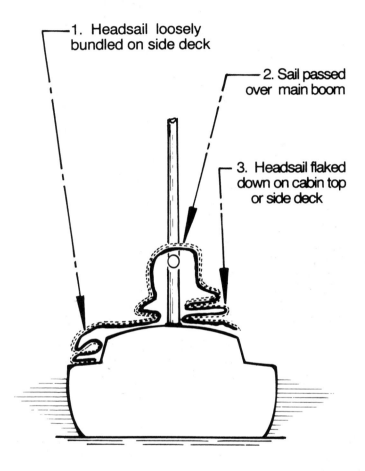

1. Headsail loosely bundled on side deck

2. Sail passed over main boom

3. Headsail flaked down on cabin top or side deck

To fold up a headsail on deck, pile the sail on one side deck, and take the foot over the top of the boom and stretch it out along the cabin top, or along the side deck, on the opposite side. The tack of the sail is normally forward, and it will usually have to be taken forward of the shrouds.

One person folds the sail in zig-zags at the fore end, and a second does the same at the aft end. If there are more people on board, one of them should carefully feed the luff of the sail over the boom at the same speed as the stowers are making the zig-zag folds. Someone else can feed the leech over at the same rate.

When there is further help available, it is often useful to have a pair of hands working halfway along the foot, making sure that the middle of the sail lies flat and snug and does not flap about in the breeze. Each person should be checking the sail, fold by fold, to make sure there are no defects that need mending.

Bagging a headsail

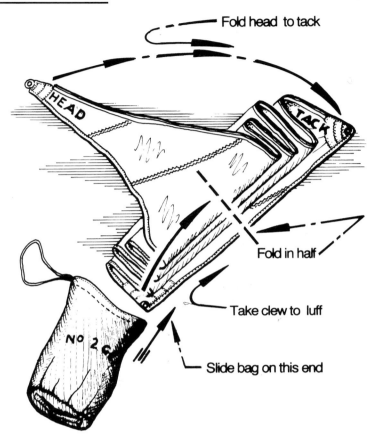

Fold head to tack

HEAD

TACK

Fold in half

Take clew to luff

Slide bag on this end

NO 2

Once a sail has been zig-zag folded, starting from the foot, there are various ways the final packing can be made, especially if the sail is to go into a traditional type of sail bag.

The technique shown here has several advantages: all the corners end up at the top of the bag, where they can be fairly easily checked for damage; and the halyard and sheets can be fixed on without taking the sail out of the bag, or at least without pulling the sail far out.

On sails that have hanks, it is sometimes possible to clip on all the hanks with the bulk of the sail still comfortably encased in the bag, and not charging about the foredeck like a demented tent. If hanking on is not possible, or fully feasible, the tack can be hooked on before the bag is taken right off, and this can be a tremendous advantage in windy weather.

These techniques work best when the bag is large, relative to the size of sail. But under-size bags, are *always* a nuisance. Most experienced owners dislike tiny bags so much that they transfer them to other duties such as holding the bosun's stores, and then they buy voluminous new bags, with a stout handle sewn on the bottom.

Stowing 'hard' sails

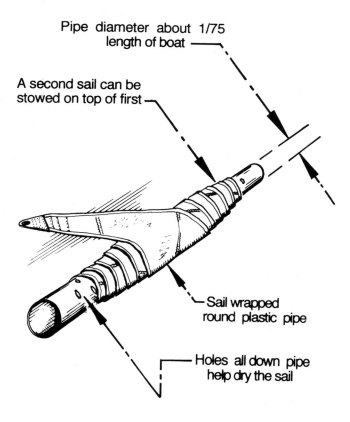

Pipe diameter about 1/75 length of boat ——

A second sail can be stowed on top of first ——

Sail wrapped round plastic pipe

Holes all down pipe help dry the sail

The type of sail that does not fold easily and is made of a cloth that is free from creases cannot be stowed in an ordinary sail bag without doing damage. For a One-design yacht, small cruiser-racer or dinghy, a convenient way to stow the sails is to wrap them round plastic piping.

The pipe has to be slightly longer than the foot of the sail, and the foot is wrapped on first. With one person at each end, the plastic tube is rotated and the sail progressively wound on. It helps if a third, and perhaps even a fourth, person steers the sail on to the tube.

The sail will, ideally, be wiped dry as it is wrapped, but this will not remove all the moisture. Holes typically 1 in (25 mm) in diameter drilled in a pattern all over the tube walls will help the drying-out process.

A sail with battens sewn into pockets must be rolled on so that the battens lie along the length of the tube. This normally means that the leech has to be at right angles to the length of the pipe, because the battens are at right angles to the leech. However, the bottom batten is often at right angles to the boom, to suit the reefing arrangements, so this lower batten may have to be taken out of its pocket before the sail is wrapped on the tube.

Packing a wet spinnaker

Wet nylon cloth clings to itself, so that a sopping spinnaker can be awkward to repack, especially in the hurly-burly of a hectic race. It is bad enough with plenty of help, but doing it single-handed can be miserable.

One way to ease the problem is to stretch the sail out, by taking the head as far forward in the boat as feasible. It can help to have a hook near the fore end of the fo'c's'le, or at least as far forward as can be reached in a hurry. If the hook is right on the forward bulkhead it may be out of reach for anyone standing on the small sole area in the bow cabin.

The sail has to be teased out, so that the clews are well separated, but this is easier if much of the sail is up forward, and the full width of the saloon can be used. It may even help to stuff one clew down the quarter berth as far as can be reached without scrambling about a lot.

Just spreading the sail out helps to get rid of some of the moisture. If the sail is not going to be used for some time, leaving it spread out will accelerate the drying-out progress. On boats with heaters this is the time to use all the race-winning facilities that are on board..... there is no rule against warming the cabin and hence drying out the spinnaker..... so that the chances of it going up next time without a snarl-up are much enhanced.

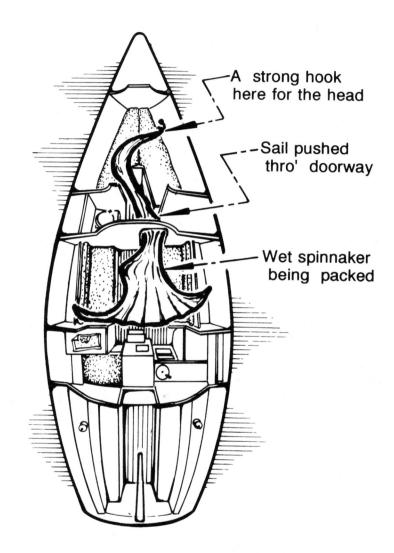

A strong hook here for the head

Sail pushed thro' doorway

Wet spinnaker being packed

Hanked headsail handling

This technique for bagging a hanked headsail suits a crew that is small in relation to the size of sail. It can be used for a sail on a luff foil, provided the luff is folded as shown when the sail comes down.

The sail is dropped fully, then both the halyard and the tack securing device taken off. A rope is passed round the sail, also through the head and tack eyes, then pulled tight..... in the illustration the crew have not got this line tight enough. At least they have pulled each luff fold to the same side.

A tier is put tightly round the middle of the sail. At least one more tier is lashed round the sail, but several may be needed on a large sail. If the sail is going to be left on deck, these tiers will pass through slots in the toerail to keep the sail away from the middle of the foredeck.

If the sail is going to be put in its bag, the clew is tucked in first, and the bag pulled over the sail from aft, then the hanks are freed off. A really voluminous bag is needed, and the majority of 'standard issue' bags are too small. The best way to get the correct size of bag is to borrow a selection from a sailmaker and try them

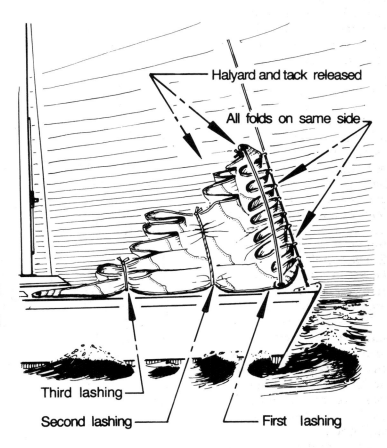

Halyard and tack released

All folds on same side

Third lashing

Second lashing

First lashing

out..... being very careful to keep them clean or the sailmaker will not accept back those that are not needed.

Another way to get the right size of bag is to secure the sail as shown in this drawing then measure the girth at the fore end, also

the fore-and-aft length after the sail has been bunched up near the forestay. Best of all, get the sailmaker on board and ask him to take these dimensions. Then if the bag turns out to be too small, there's no doubt who is to blame!

Tabarly technique for large headsails

For a singlehander, the prospect of having a genoa streaming overboard as it is raised or lowered is a serious worry. Even quite large crews have moments of crisis during these manoeuvres. This simple trick, invented by Eric Tabarly, is an adaptation of the device sometimes used to prevent a spinnaker winding itself round the forestay. It keeps the headsail inboard and more or less under control, rather like a set of lazyjacks on a mainsail.

The 'net' has to be rigged before any work starts on the headsail. Any forward halyard can be used, though it will normally be easiest to use the spinnaker one. Since the load on the 'net' is light, the ropes that make it up can be quite light, and ¼ or ⅜ in (6 or 8 mm) should suit most yachts.

The upper joins can be bowlines, and the lower ends of all the lines are secured at roughly equal intervals along the toe rail, inboard of the guard rail wires. These ropes can be secured further inboard, on cleats for instance, and the aft one can be at the mast foot.

As with so many things, the best way to try this

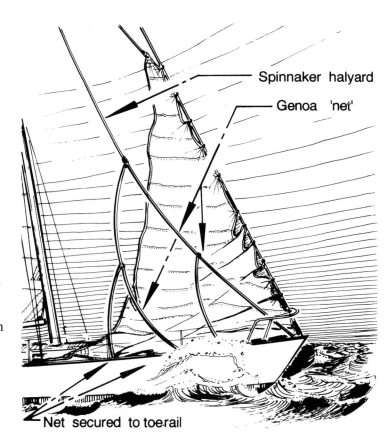

Spinnaker halyard

Genoa 'net'

Net secured to toe rail

device is first in fine weather, in daylight, with the whole procedure talked through. Next it should be used in moderate weather, when going to windward in a lumpy sea. When the 'net' is needed in fierce conditions, plenty of previous practice will ensure there are no snarl-ups.

8. Sail Covers and Bags

Mainsail cover fastenings

The top drawing shows a cross-section of the boom with a stowed mainsail under a cover that is hooked up along the bottom.

Some sailmakers use special plastic hooks to secure sail covers along the edges. Also available are matching plastic eyes. The securing part of these fastenings are thin flat 'plates' that are attached by a sewing machine using a zig-zag stitch.

If hooks and eyes are used, the sail cover has to be a neat fit, and if the sail is changed, perhaps to a fully battened one, the cover may no longer fit. However, if hooks alone are used, sewn to both bottom edges, a light line or shock cord pulls the edges together, leaving a good ventilation slot along the full length. With this arrangement the cover will fit different sails, and can be pulled tight so that it does not flap in a gale.

On yachts that have a small crew, this arrangement, with a lashing full length along the bottom, is good because it is not always possible to stow the sail in the tidiest way. There may be some bulkiness in the sail, or the head may be folded further aft than usual. This type of open-bottomed cover copes with these problems easily.

Hooks can be used on an old sail cover that needs enlarging or repairing. Because the hooks are plastic and put on with a sewing machine, they are not expensive, and can give an aged cover an extra year or two of life.

These plastic hooks and eyes have other uses on board, such as on sailcloth containers in the cabin used for stowing clothes, on spinnaker bags, on curtains, and so on.

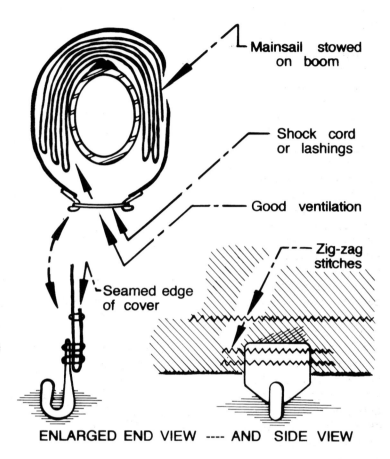

Mainsail stowed on boom

Shock cord or lashings

Good ventilation

Zig-zag stitches

Seamed edge of cover

ENLARGED END VIEW ---- AND SIDE VIEW

Numbers on sail covers

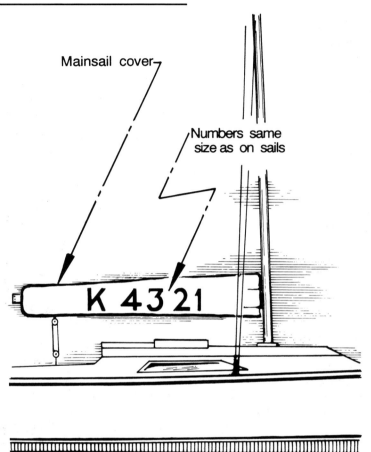

Mainsail cover

Numbers same
size as on sails

K 4321

There are lots of good reasons why mainsail covers should have the yacht's racing number stitched on. It helps identification when the boat is in a marina or on a mooring; it reduces the chances of the yacht being stolen; it ensures that when the cover is sent for repairs, the right one gets back to the correct boat, and so on. Some craft have the boat's name on the sail cover, but this is usually more expensive as sailmakers normally charge by the individual figure or letter.

Just as useful, if the yacht loses a digit off a sail during a race series, one can be unstitched from the cover and sewn on to the sail. For this reason, the numbers should not be the self-adhesive type, because they are so hard to peel off.

In long-distance races the rules often require every yacht to carry a length of cloth with the sail number on, for displaying when crossing the finishing line, or in an emergency when the sails are all down. To save having a special piece of cloth, the sail cover can be used.

Safer sail bag

In good weather and bad, sail bags get lost overboard. Sometimes the reason is that one person working alone on the foredeck does not have enough hands to hold on to the sail, halyard, sheets and bag all at once. Sometimes there are two people on the foredeck, and each thinks the other has lashed the sail bag safely in place. Sometimes the bag goes overboard with the sail still inside it!

The ideal way to secure the sail bag is by the two bottom corners; this makes it easier to get the sail in or out. If the sail is being put back, it's often best to have the bag lashed to the lee toerail. The uphill wind-ward side is used if the sail is being hauled out of the bag..... in each case, gravity helps with the work. This matters if the sail is heavy, and doubly so if there is a shortage of hands for the job.

To make the bag easy to secure, take two small chocks of wood and push them right into the bottom corners of the bag. Put a tight lashing round the out-side of the bag, trapping the chocks in place, as shown in the enlarged detail. The chocks can be made of something like ½ in (12 mm) marine ply about

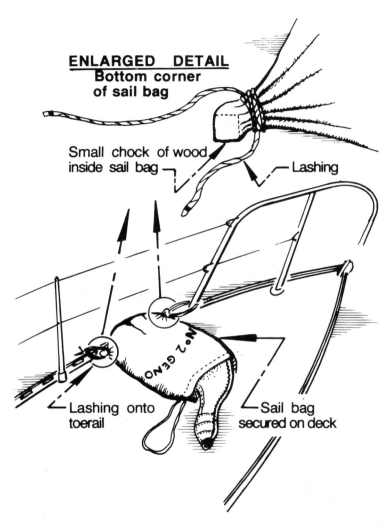

ENLARGED DETAIL
Bottom corner of sail bag

Small chock of wood inside sail bag

Lashing

Lashing onto toerail

Sail bag secured on deck

1 x 1 in (25 x 25 mm) for every 23 ft (7 m) of boat length.

This trick can be used in other places. For instance, if away on a cruise, far from repair facilities, and the mainsail cover loses a corner eye, a temporary lashing can be secured using a small chock of wood.

Sail bag for rough weather

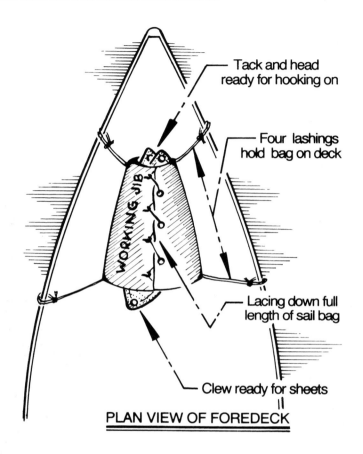

Tack and head
ready for hooking on

Four lashings
hold bag on deck

WORKING JIB

Lacing down full
length of sail bag

Clew ready for sheets

PLAN VIEW OF FOREDECK

This is not really a sail 'bag', more of a 'tunnel' tapered at each end, with a slit all down the length. The folded sail has its head and tack protruding at one end, and the clew at the other, so the halyard and tack can be secured while the sail is still inside the bag. The sheets can also be tied on, after the bag has been laid on the foredeck and its four lash-ings knotted on to the toerails or the stanchion bases.

When the time comes to hoist the sail, the lacing is undone and the sail hanked on. Some of the hanks, possibly all of them, can be secured by undoing just the fore end of the lacing, provided that the sail is correctly folded inside its 'tunnel bag'.

For small sails, instead of a lacing there can be shock cord that loops over hooks sewn to the opposite side of the slit along the top of the bag. The name of the sail should be marked on the bag, and if there is more than one of this type, they should be different colours so that the correct one is easy to find in a dimly lit fore cabin or cockpit locker.

Spinnaker bag details

The name of each spinnaker should be marked on four sides of the bag, so that when it is put ready for hoisting the whole crew can see that the correct sail has been brought on deck. The lettering must be large enough for all to read, even by the helmsman who is well aft and may be wearing glasses covered in spray.

Depending on the hoisting technique being used, the clips on the bag have to be secured to suit the available hooking-on points. Most crews like the bag to be secured tight down on the deck, so the bottom snap hook must be positioned to clip on to the toe rail. The upper one often goes on to the lower lifeline, so the hook has to be on tapes stitched above the wire to cope with the upward pull on the bag when the sail is hauled up.

So that the spinnaker goes aloft swiftly under the pull of the halyard, the draw-string on the top of the bag must be very slack. Often it is taken right off, and some sailmakers never fit a drawstring on a spinnaker bag. The bag shown here has a lid that folds over, with a piece of cloth forming a hinge. The closure is by three or more strips of Velcro. Just how many strips

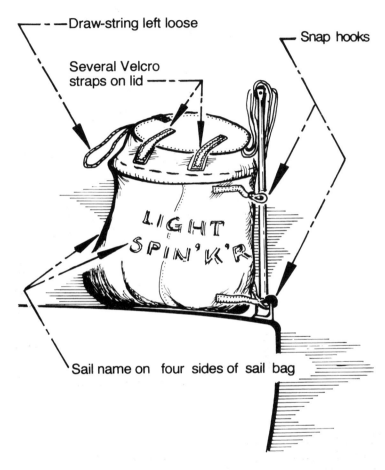

Draw-string left loose

Several Velcro straps on lid

Snap hooks

LIGHT SPIN'K'R

Sail name on four sides of sail bag

of Velcro, and how wide they are, depends on experience, the size of the sail, and the strength of the wind. In heavy weather no one wants the sail to escape from its bag too soon.

As a crude guide, there should be at least three strips of Velcro, and one more is added for every extra 10 ft (3 m) of boat's length over 30 ft (9 m). This Velcro should be about 2 in (5 cm) wide with the same length of contact.

Super spinnaker bag

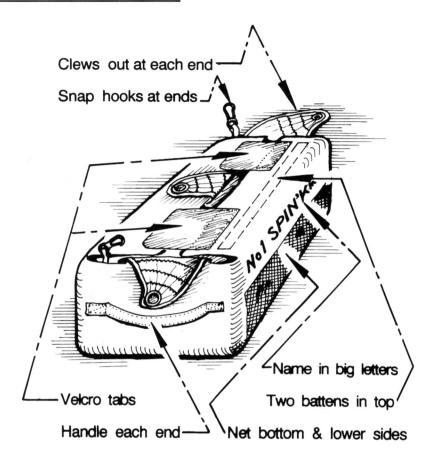

Clews out at each end

Snap hooks at ends

No1 SPIN'R

Name in big letters

Velcro tabs

Two battens in top

Handle each end

Net bottom & lower sides

A spinnaker bag that is wide and squat is easy to pack quickly. The top of this version opens full length with flaps that fold right back to make the whole bag accessible. These flaps are kept shut by two tabs of sail bag material which act as covers for the Velcro patches.

When the sail is packed, the head is out in the middle of the top slot, and each clew has a full-width slot at the end of the bag. Normally there will be a 'dog's lead' type snap clip on top of each end, but some people prefer these hooks to be at the bottom as well.

To keep the bag rigid and easy to pack there are flat fibreglass battens stitched inside along each top flap, and also stiff grab handles at each end. The name or number of the sail is marked boldly on each long side. A net bottom that extends halfway up each long side promotes quick drying and ventilation.

The one defect of this rather special bag is its high cost. But if it helps to win races, it is cheap at almost any price.

Altering under-size sail bags

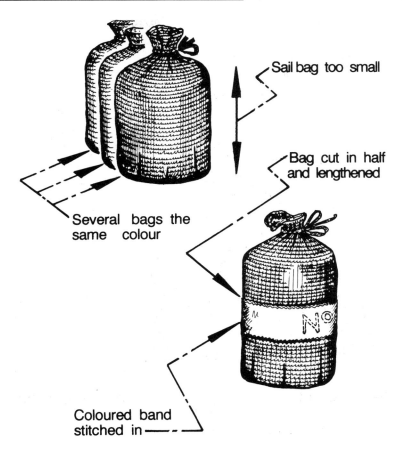

Sail bag too small

Bag cut in half and lengthened

Several bags the same colour

Coloured band stitched in

After a fine weekend cruise it is no fun trying to stuff sails back into bags that are too small. Buying new bags is seldom cost effective, especially as it is so easy to enlarge a sail bag.

The empty bag is laid flat and carefully cut 'across the waist'. The two pieces are pulled apart, and a broad band of cloth sewn in. The sail's name and number can be stencilled or indelibly written in bold letters two or three times round the new band.

Some sailmakers dispatch all their products in sail bags of the same colour, or with some minimal distinguishing feature such as a thin strip of mutely coloured cloth round the outside of the bag. In a dimly lit fore cabin or cavernous cockpit locker, it can be hard to tell one bag from another. A new, broad, brightly coloured band round the middle of each sail bag makes all the difference in these circumstances. If the bags are stowed upright, it will probably be best to have the newly sewn-in strips near the top.

There is an added bonus: sails that are not tightly jammed into bags dry faster.

Sail changing in heavy weather

Simple alterations can be made to an ordinary sail bag to make work on the foredeck easier. If there is no grab handle on the bottom of the bag, this is the first thing to add. A couple of lengths of rope tied to the handle are needed to tie the bag down, usually to the toerail, but sometimes to a mooring cleat or pulpit leg.

Tying even the simplest knot when the foredeck is hurtling up and down like a demented lift can be nearly impossible, and some people prefer to have short lines on the bottom of the bag with snap shackles on the end. Worn snap shackles that are no longer safe on spinnaker sheets are normally entirely adequate in this location. They may not be large enough to snap round the leg of a pulpit, so the rope is passed right round the leg, and the snap shackle clipped on to the rope.

So that the sail can be hanked on while still in the bag, a slit is made down from the top of the bag. Hooks and eyes are stitched each side of the slit, and these are progressively opened up to allow the halyard to be secured, the tack hauled out and fixed down, and often the hanks

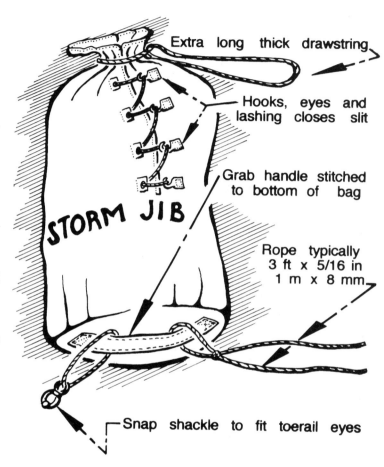

can be clipped on the forestay while the bulk of the sail stays snugly encased and docile.

Tidy cockpit, safe cockpit

Whether cruising or racing, the cockpit tends to be too small and too full of people, gear and, above all, ropes. What is needed is somewhere secure for the coiled mainsheet and stowage for things like race instructions, a bar of chocolate, a flashlight, and so on.

A bag slung under a main horse track which extends across the cockpit at seat level works well. The depth of the bag will normally be slightly less than the depth of the cockpit well, so that water tumbling aboard drains away quickly and does not get trapped by the bag. The container width is often about the same as the distance across the well. If in doubt, the best way forward is to coil the rope and see how much volume it occupies.

The pouch for the race instructions may have a transparent face so that the information can be read without taking the paper out of its stowage. A flap lid over the pouch will keep rain off, but the contents will eventually get wet, so drain holes are essential.

Sometimes the drain holes will just be cut or 'hot-knifed' in the material; sometimes they will be eyelets hammered in. No hole should be less than ½ in

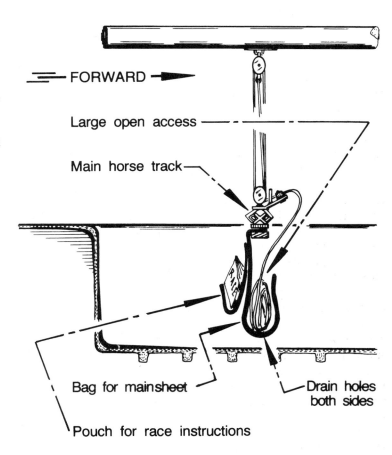

FORWARD →

Large open access

Main horse track

Bag for mainsheet

Pouch for race instructions

Drain holes both sides

(12 mm) diameter, otherwise it may get blocked by debris.

This sort of made-to-measure rope holder can be bought from most local sailmakers. Some sailmakers will take the dimensions on the boat, others will ask the

owner for the size. The former will probably charge a fair bit more!

Simple stowage bags from sail material

Sailmakers can put together furniture for the cockpit or cabin more quickly and cheaply than shipwrights. The two-compartment stowage bag shown here (top left) is designed to fasten on to the lining in the fore cabin, or go in the cockpit, or by a berth without reducing the sleeper's comfort (see bottom left). In practice, if the bags are filled with soft clothing, the comfort of the berth is improved as the sleeper is not thrown against the hard hull lining in rough weather.

The first job is to measure the space. It is best to make the back of the bag (shown top right) slightly smaller than the area available. The bag is held to the ship's lining by at least three screws through a wood batten about 1½ x ⅜ in (40 x 10 mm). Round-head 10 gauge screws with washers under the heads are used.

The back of the bag has an extra 2½ in (65 mm) depth to form the seam for the batten. The front piece needs to be turned over and seamed at the top, so when finished it has 2½ in (65 mm) less height than the back. This seam may contain shock cord to pull the bag tight at the top.

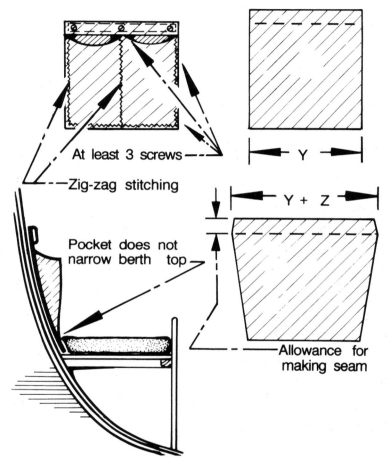

At least 3 screws

Zig-zag stitching

Pocket does not narrow berth top

Y

Y + Z

Allowance for making seam

The top of the front is greater than the width of the top of the back by the measurement Z. This dimension Z gives the bag ample capacity and Z is about one quarter of Y which is the width of the bag. The material used may be Terylene/Dacron, coloured acrylic cloth, or PVC.

Safer roller headsails on moorings

During a prolonged spell of strong winds, a few roller furling headsails come unfurled. Sometimes the furling line chafes through or gets adrift from the drum. Sometimes it is left unsecured, and then the windage on the sheets is enough to start the headsail unfurling. Once the wind can fill the clew corner of the sail, it worries away till the whole sail is unfurled, and then all sorts of troubles arise. The yacht starts sailing round her mooring, or heeling dangerously and snatching at her warps if she is in a marina. The yacht's owner will be lucky if he only has a damaged sail.

As a safety precaution, a sailmaker should be asked to stitch a short length of tape to the bottom of the sail at the correct angle, which is easy to mark on the sail when it is furled up. This tough tape has an eye or loop in the end, to which a short length of rope is attached. The rope is secured round a convenient cleat or bollard, or through an eye in the toerail or some such. This rope should be tight, and strong enough to prevent the sail from unfurling regardless of the hurricane's blast. This is such a simple precaution to take before leaving the yacht, and it may prevent a lot of damage.

The drawing shows the sheets coming off the port side of the furled sail so the safety tape must come off the starboard side.

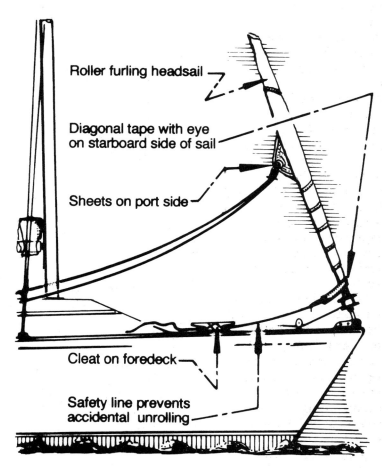

Roller furling headsail

Diagonal tape with eye on starboard side of sail

Sheets on port side

Cleat on foredeck

Safety line prevents accidental unrolling

Luff foil preserver

When a boat is laid up with the mast standing the luff foil will vibrate and wear, even when the wind is blowing quite gently. On the moorings the foil can jutter and shudder so much that the boat responds, and a sympathetic reaction in the hull is felt

To keep the luff foil still, sailmakers produce tiny headsails that slide up about one-fifth of the length of the foil from the bottom. The sheets are hauled taut and secured. To prevent the headsail sheets from weathering, special sheets are used on the best-organised boats.

The proportions of this sail are roughly the same as on a working jib with high-cut foot. The sail must be small because it must not have any 'drive' in it – otherwise in very severe conditions it will cause the yacht to sail round her moorings..... or topple over if she is ashore. As a rough guide, most people favour a luff length of about 1 ft (30 cm) for every 30 ft (9 m) of yacht length. It is widely agreed that the size of the micro-sail must be as small as possible. Just as important, if the yacht is stored ashore she must be in a very sheltered location and extremely well propped

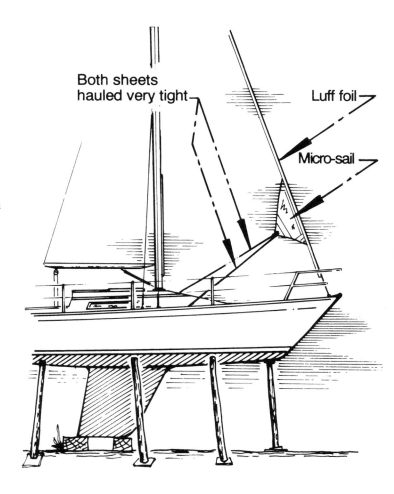

up (with a minimum of seven shores each side) if she has one of these micro-sails set. Nearly everyone agrees that masts should be down when yachts are ashore, and it cannot be over-emphasised that for a boat that is hauled up, this micro-sail should never be used if the yacht is even slightly exposed to windy conditions.

Snarl-free leech line

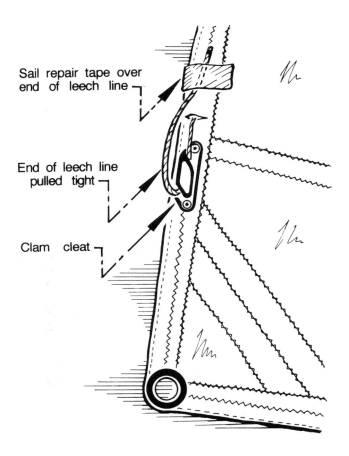

Sail repair tape over end of leech line ⌐

End of leech line pulled tight ⌐

Clam cleat ⌐

The leech line on any sail is a potential mischief maker. Sometimes headsail leech lines catch on shrouds when tacking, and some find their way into sheet lead blocks at inconvenient moments. What is needed is a simple, safe arrangement that makes it easy for the crew to adjust the line, but also reduces the chances of foul-ups.

One well-established technique is to have a clam cleat riveted to the sail close to the point where the line emerges from its seam. This will hold the line well, provided the end of the 'string' is secured safely. Some crews take the line down through the clew eye, and back up the leech where the line is knotted on to itself.

Another way of holding the end of the line is with a length of sail repair tape, or several pieces of duct tape. These sticky tapes tend to need renewing frequently, and are not reliable in wet weather.

A few sailmakers sew a pocket on to the sail to take the surplus line. This little pouch may have a closure flap at the top, complete with Velcro strip to hold the pocket closed.

Safe chafe patches

When fitting doubler patches to protect a sail against chafe it is tempting to use cloth with a self-adhesive backing. This material is carried on well-equipped yachts for making temporary repairs, and is so easy to use.

However, the sticky backing is not long-lasting and reliable; after a time, the edges peel up. There has been at least one instance when a patch held only by self-adhesive glue started to come off a genoa in the middle of the night. Unnoticed in the dark, the patch wrapped itself round the shroud, and when the time came to tack, the leech of the headsail was firmly secured to the shroud, so tacking was impossible.

The wind was getting up, and there were only two people on board. They had a considerable problem cutting the patch free from the shroud where it was wrapped round many times. There was first the acute difficulty of getting up to the outboard end of the leeward crosstrees. Next, the cloth was hard to cut through as it was so tightly wrapped round the thin wire.

To avoid this sort of trouble, all anti-chafe patches should be double stitched all round using zig-zag stitching.

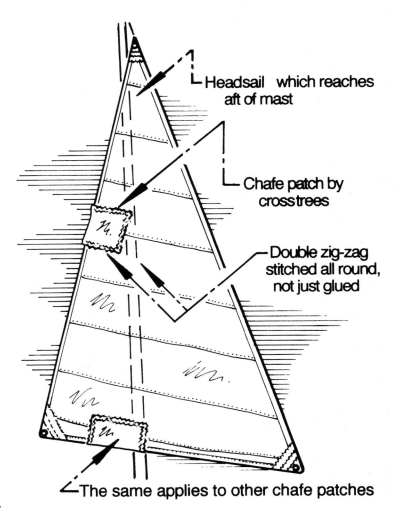

Headsail which reaches aft of mast

Chafe patch by crosstrees

Double zig-zag stitched all round, not just glued

The same applies to other chafe patches

Reefing precautions

Sail troubles mostly occur in bad weather, and reefing is a time when sails are damaged. If the reefing pennant breaks or stretches badly, the sail may be torn at the reef points. In practice, a reef pennant is most likely to break when there is an extra-strong squall, or when the reef is being hauled down. These are times when a breaking rope causes the maximum crises, so it is well worth checking reef ropes every month, and using extra-strong lines.

Many experienced sailors put an additional lashing through the leech reef eye and round the boom after the reef has been taken in. It reduces the loading on the pennant, pulls the sail down to the boom, and is a sensible precaution against pennant failure.

The leech of a reefed mainsail has always been vulnerable to chafe, as a study of a hundred mainsails will show. When reefing a laminated sail, or any modern 'hi-tech' sail that has protective outer layers, it is doubly important to make sure the sail is not jammed under a rope, or pinched against the boom. As the reef pennant is hauled tight one of the crew has to ensure the sail is kept clear of all dangers.

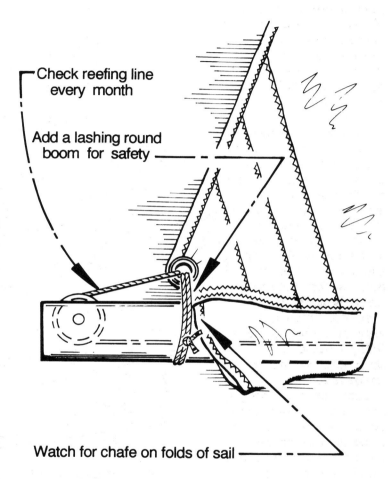

Check reefing line every month

Add a lashing round boom for safety

Watch for chafe on folds of sail

After the second or third reef has been taken in, it makes sense to take a light lashing through the first reef leech eye and through the eye that has been tightened down. This prevents the sail from flogging about and chafing itself. It is important that this line is freed off before the reef is let go.

Eliminating topping lift wear

If the topping lift lies on the windward side of the mainsail, it will wear the sail's stitching from top to bottom. As this rope tends to work over a fairly narrow band of the sail, the wear is usually over a short length of each seam. When the topping lift has become hardened with age, it can chafe seriously in just one lengthy voyage. It will chafe the lee side often enough, so getting the rope to leeward is no guarantee that there will be no damage.

The obvious way to get rid of this problem is to have both ends of the topping lift secured at the foot of the mast when under way. However, this presents problems when the time comes to reef or take the sail down. The topping lift has to be taken to the aft end of the boom for these operations. It is therefore necessary to have the end of the boom fitted with a large accessible loop, and the topping lift end must have a big, easily worked snap shackle. Anyone reaching up to fix the aft end of the topping lift on to the boom should wear a safety harness.

The boom loop can be made of a length of stainless steel rigging wire, with

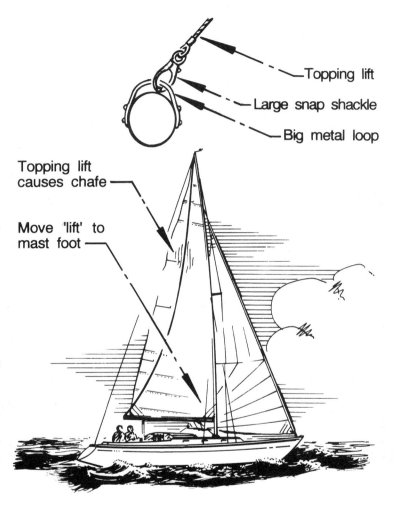

Topping lift

Large snap shackle

Big metal loop

Topping lift causes chafe

Move 'lift' to mast foot

an eye at each end bolted on to the boom. There must be big washers on the bolt heads to keep the eyes on.

Provided the boat is under about 33 ft (10 m)

the snap shackle can be the 'dog lead' type that is easy to use with one hand. It has to be big to be strong enough, and it may clang on the tubular boom.

Bagnall-Wild lazyjacks

Lazyjacks make handling the mainsail so much easier. They prevent the sail going wild or billowing off to leeward when hoisting, lowering or reefing. For a singlehander, they are one of the best aids to on-deck work.

However, they normally cause a lot of chafe, especially at the stitching on the seams. Ralph Bagnall-Wild has invented this simple improvement to eliminate this unwanted wear. He rigs the lazyjacks, like topping lifts, from near the aft end of the boom, port and starboard.

The lead of the starboard one is easy to follow on the drawing: it goes from near the boom end, starboard side, up over a block under the starboard crosstree, down to a block near the deck on the aft side of the mast, then it becomes the port lazyjack as it rises up the port side of the mast to a block under the port crosstree, and down aft to near the boom end on the port side.

The secondary lazyjacks are secured to the boom and the main lazyjacks, dividing the length of the boom into equal parts. The block at the mast-foot can be hauled down to tighten the lazyjacks. The whole system is wonderfully self-adjusting. In all weathers the lee lazyjacks blow off to leeward clear of the sail, and so cause no wear. The sail curves away from the windward ones, so they cannot chafe. The lazyjacks 'tack' or 'gybe' themselves when the mainsail tacks or gybes.

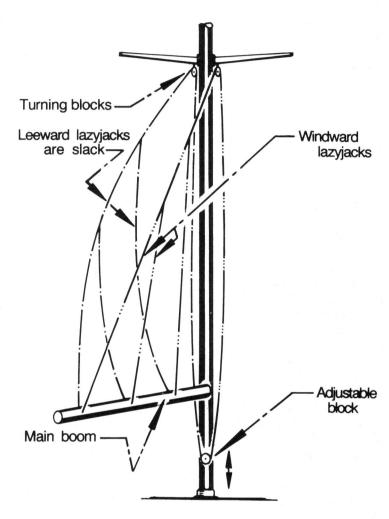

Turning blocks

Leeward lazyjacks are slack

Windward lazyjacks

Adjustable block

Main boom

Faster work, less wear

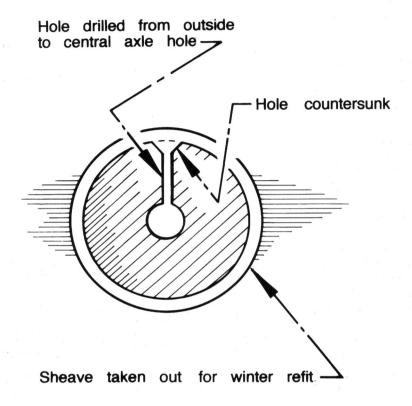

Hole drilled from outside
to central axle hole

Hole countersunk

Sheave taken out for winter refit

Whatever the job, whether it is hauling up a sail or sheeting it in, or trimming it, there is at least one sheave involved. Where there is a sheave there is effort, and to reduce effort there is nothing like a little oil.

However, getting oil into the central hole of a sheave can be difficult. Sheaves that can be removed from the mast, boom or block can have their axles greased, and this works well. But most people do not want to dismantle sheaves in the middle of the season, whereas they may want to introduce more lubrication.

If a drill is driven from the outside of each sheave to the middle hole, and then this new passageway is countersunk at the outer end, it is easy to get oil right to the axle. The sheave must not be given this treatment while it is on its axle, because the drill will dimple down into the axle.

Before reassembly, the whole sheave must be carefully cleaned to get rid of the metal shavings and swarf. Ample oil on the axle should prevent an alloy sheave from seizing on a stainless steel axle, which is an added benefit.

Numbers and letters on sails

Like much in sailmaking, there are conventions that lay down the way numbers should be put on sails. These pseudo laws largely come from racing rules, and are based on years of experience and common sense.

The numbers must never be exactly opposite one another on the two sides of the sail because when the sun shines through, none of the numbers will be recognisable.

On many sails it is quite a problem getting all the numbers and letters to fit, especially as (for instance) the traditional 'K' for Great Britain has been replaced by 'GBR'. Because there must be a space between each letter, three letters take up much more area than three times that occupied by one letter.

To use the available area to best advantage, the letters and numbers are aligned with the sail seams. No one wants to fit a number over the uneven surface of a seam, however flat and smooth the overlapped material may be. It is hard enough keeping numbers on in all weathers, without starting off at a disadvantage.

Numbers and letters tend to be self-adhesive, though some are stencilled on.

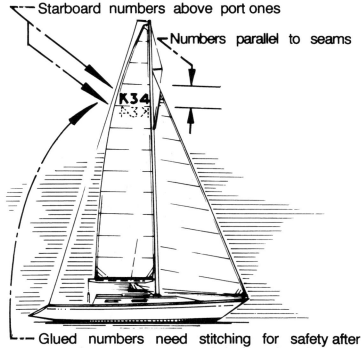

Starboard numbers above port ones

Numbers parallel to seams

K34

Glued numbers need stitching for safety after about two years and before laundering

After a time the glue begins to weaken, especially at the corners, so numbers then have to be secured with a row of zig-zag stitching all round.

Stencilled numbers wear off, especially at folds and where anything can chafe.

A wire that sweeps across a sail a few times will scrape off a stencilled number, often leaving a sort of speckled scattering of colour, just illegible enough for a sharp racing competitor to use for a protest.

Restitching a sail to extend its life

When a sail is well liked but well worn, the owner has a dilemma. Does he order an identical one, knowing that even with modern technology the replacement may not be quite as good, or does he try and get more use from the existing sail? Part of the problem is that, thanks to modern techniques, a replacement sail can be markedly different from the one it is replacing because the person who programs the computer may press one wrong key and the mistake goes undetected.

So far as costs go, extending a sail's life may save money in the short term, but restitching still costs cash, and the life extension may not be more than a year or two.

Restitching varies from one sail loft to another. Some sailmakers take off all the corners, batten pockets, the headboard, the reef doublers, and so on. They fit new corners, maybe a new headboard, and so on. Other sail lofts just leave most of the sail as they find it, and stitch down the middle of each seam as far as convenient and possible.

Restitching is carried out between the two existing rows of zig-zagging. Some seamstresses use a matching

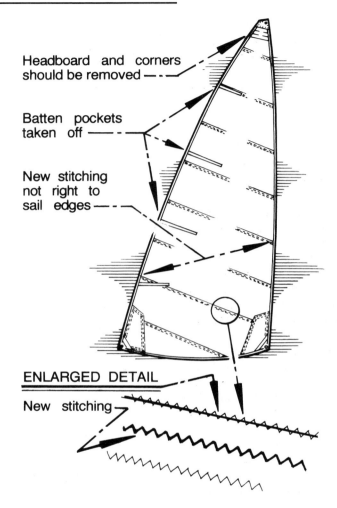

Headboard and corners should be removed

Batten pockets taken off

New stitching not right to sail edges

ENLARGED DETAIL

New stitching

thread so that few people realise the sail has been reworked. Some use a contrasting thread that is easier to see, and to ensure that no length of seam is missed out in the renewal process. (See the enlarged detail in the drawing.)

This technique costs well under half the price of a

new sail because, apart perhaps from some corners, little new material is used. With a big sail the process is difficult because such a large bulk of sail has to be worked under the arm of the sewing machine. Like so much in sailmaking, there are lots of reasons for and against restitching.

Curing leech flutter

A fluttering leech is doubly annoying because it is inefficient and noisy. The rattling crackle can be so loud that it is hard to concentrate on deck. The first course of action is to tighten the leech line. This can make the problem worse, and it may cause the leech to curl back..... a picture of inefficiency.

There are two full cures: the trailing edge of the sail may be sliced off, or the aft ends of the seams can be 'tightened' by increasing the cloth overlaps as shown in the drawing. In practice, more than three seams may have to be 'tightened'. The job involves slicing through the stitching inwards from the leech for perhaps half the length of the seam. New lines are drawn on the sail to show where the cloth edge is to go, and the seams are stitched up to these lines. This gives an increase in the amount that one cloth overlaps the adjacent one.

In the drawing, the third seam from the top has an extra overlap of X millimetres (or inches for that matter). The fourth seam down is typically given 50 per cent more overlap, ie 1.5 X. The fifth seam down is given the same extra overlap as the third.

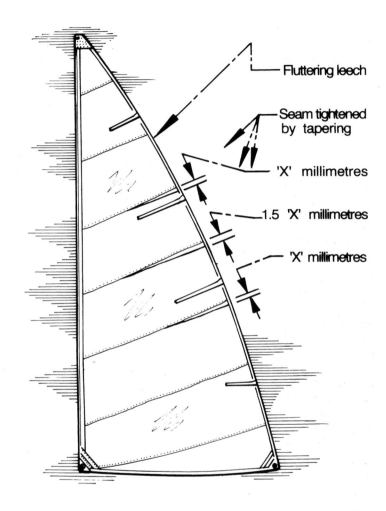

Fluttering leech

Seam tightened by tapering

'X' millimetres

1.5 'X' millimetres

'X' millimetres

This is an area where a sailmaker's skill and experience is essential.

However, a rattling juddering leech may mean that the sail is so old that it is due for replacement, especially if the sail is discoloured, chafed, and peppered with patches.

Leech flutter may mean that the person who designed the sail was too greedy for area, and made the round of the roach too big. Slicing a sliver off the leech may be the answer, especially if the sail is used for cruising where the total area is not critical.

Curing clew defects

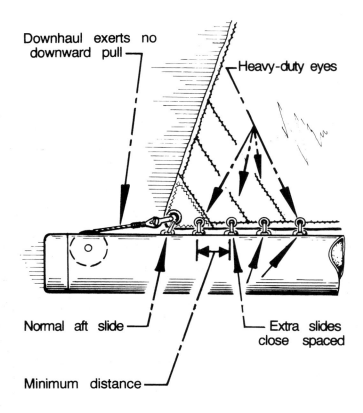

Downhaul exerts no downward pull

Heavy-duty eyes

Normal aft slide

Minimum distance

Extra slides close spaced

Many mainsail outhauls pull the sail almost horizontally along the boom. However, the tension in this area is largely up the leech, so the aft slide has to carry a big load. If an ordinary slide is fitted on the foot near the clew, it often gives trouble.

There are special long slides available for this location, but they are not always available and, when they are, they may be inadequate on their own. Sometimes two of these extra-long slides are fitted, but even a single one can be expensive.

One economical solution that will last and survive involves fitting hydraulically pressed eyes along the foot, close together, with slides at each one to share the load. These slides should be made of metal not plastic, especially for long-range cruising.

The application of a little waterproof grease on the track at the aft end is worth trying, though the grease must not be so thick that it soils the sail. The sail will have thick layers of cloth at the corner, but occasionally additional strengthening may be needed, notably at the forward of these new slides.

Typical mainsail wear

Because the head of the mainsail is far above the deck, damage is not noticed when the sail is aloft. The top of the sail is highly stressed as the wind is stronger at the top of the mast than at the bottom. Also, the sail narrows to a small width that has to contain all the strains in a limited area. It is no wonder that near the head-board there is often plenty of damage, even before the end of the summer.

The headboard has a bushed eye to take the main halyard shackle. The hole may wear or be crushed by a small shackle, so that a new 'lining' or bushing in the hole may be needed. In extreme cases of wear, a new headboard has to be fitted.

When the headboard rivets corrode it is usually easy to drill them out and fit new ones, but the replacements may have to be one size larger. Worn stitching is no problem; it just needs a run or two of the sewing machine over the affected area. The machine cannot work right up to the edge of the head-board, but this seldom matters, as the rivets through the two sides of the headboard act like secure stitching.

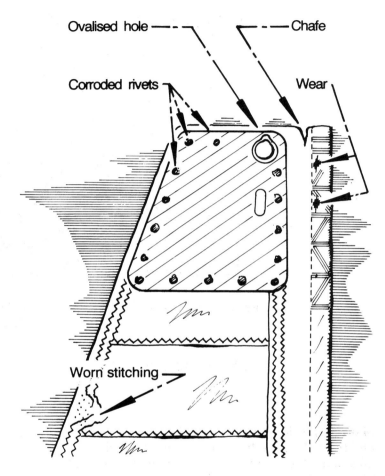

Wear on the cloth round the top of the luff rope is common, and must not be allowed to continue other-wise the sail and the rope may part. Likewise, chafe right at the top cannot be neglected. Sometimes it is necessary to take the head-board off to do a proper repair job in this area, and if the headboard is less than perfect it makes sense to fit a new one.

Repairing headboard rivets

Corroding rivets are common. The way to repair them is to drill them out and fit the next size up in the slightly enlarged holes. Sometimes the holes do not get enlarged, and the same size of rivet is put in. There are various circumstances when it is better to drill new holes between the existing rivets, and fit new fastenings.

For instance, if only smaller rivets are available, the existing holes will be too big. Then again, when far away from facilities, offshore cruising in remote regions, it may be necessary to use bolts with clenched-on nuts instead of rivets. Incidentally, copper clenches should never be used in aluminium alloy headboards because serious corrosion will result.

Offshore with no power drill on board, it may be easier to make new holes and fit rivets in these holes. Whereas it is easy to drill through aluminium, it can be difficult to drill out old steel rivets.

The number of new rivets need not be quite as many as the old ones provided they are properly tightened and fit well, but they should be spread all over, with the emphasis round the perimeter.

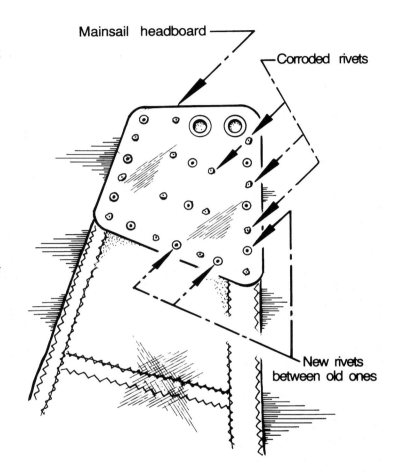

Mainsail headboard

Corroded rivets

New rivets between old ones

Repairing a damaged corner

This simple technique for dealing with a damaged corner only works if the trouble is spotted before it has become serious. It will cope with an old-fashioned 'ring-and-turnover' type of corner, or a modern hydraulically pressed one. It is a temporary repair to deal with all sorts of failures, from corrosion to elongation.

In the drawing two pieces of tape have been used for the repair, but three or even four pieces can be sewn in place, according to the size of the corner and the amount of space. The tapes are made long enough to extend far from the corner, possibly to near the perimeter of the doubling.

It is hard and sometimes impossible to hand-stitch through many layers of cloth, so tape A on top of the sail is to the left of tape A on the underside. And tape B is clear of tape A and also not sewn on to itself on the other side.

It is probable that the tape will need folding or pinching in sideways at the ring, but this does not matter. The first tape is sewn on one side of the sail, then passed through the eye. On the other side of the sail, the tape must be held tightly against the ring while it is sewn. Various techniques can be used to do this.

One way to hold the tape tight is to bend the sail slightly as if about to fold it, and sew the end of the tape, then work towards the eye. As the stitches extend towards the corner the sail is pulled on to the tape, tightening the latter.

Another trick is to hold the tape with a Mole grip, before stitching it. Alternatively, the tape can be pulled tight and secured locally with Superglue before stitching it.

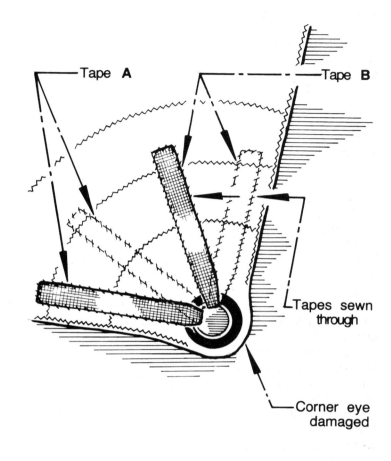

Tape A

Tape B

Tapes sewn through

Corner eye damaged

Common corner problems

Normal wear and tear on sails is regularly found in the same places, regardless of who made the sail, or the type of yacht. These usual wear spots include the batten pockets, the areas of the mainsail and mizzens that touch the crosstrees, and all corners.

This drawing shows the sort of wear that occasionally occurs in a few weeks, though it usually takes at least a full summer. These troubles are often found if a sail has been subject to prolonged use in bad weather.

The corner patches stand out from a sail so they tend to be easily chafed. Only one row of stitching is shown along each edge, but a sail that is going to be hard-used needs at least two rows..... and three is far better. When one row of stitching is chafed it is only common sense to look at adjacent lines of sewing and expect to find trouble there too. This applies all over a sail.

The tape on the edge extending round the corner is vulnerable, especially if it has a single row of straight-line stitches. When the corner eye takes a beating, this tape usually shares the grief.

Modern eyes do not stretch to an oval shape anything like as much as the old bronze type. Sometimes the eye starts to come out of the hole made for it in the multiple layers of cloth, and occasionally barbed metal teeth are exposed. These problems, or ovalising, or any form of distortion, are a clear sign that the eye is no longer reliable and needs replacing.

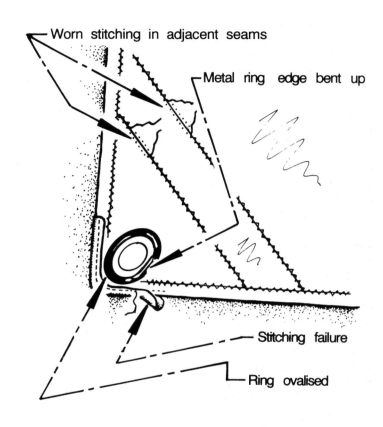

Worn stitching in adjacent seams

Metal ring edge bent up

Stitching failure

Ring ovalised

Mending a torn corner

If the corner of a sail tears right off, it is seldom possible to put a new eye in at sea. What is needed is some swiftly applied replacement that can be used for securing the corner. An ideal answer is two or three loops of strong tapes, sewn repeatedly through and through. The tapes can be sail tier material, or strong tape carried on board specially for this sort of repair, or even short lengths of rope. However, the latter is not so easy to sew on effectively.

The sewing has to be extensive, and reach well away from the corner. As a rough guide, the length of tape sewn each side of the sail should be at least 2 per cent of the luff length. The loop or eye has to be just large enough to take the halyard shackle, or tack snap shackle or sheet bowlines..... according to which eye has been torn out. If in doubt, it is better to make the loops too large.

Heavy-duty sail needles and a sailmaker's palm are needed, as well as waxed thread, used double. The corner of the sail may be too thick to get the needle through. If this is the problem, a nail or sharp-pointed tool is hammered through the sail to make a series of

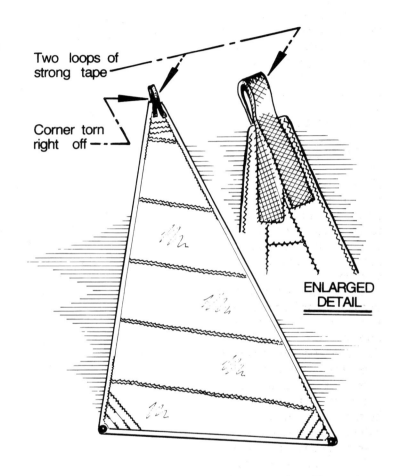

Two loops of strong tape

Corner torn right off

ENLARGED DETAIL

holes. On a Terylene or Dacron sail a row of holes can be made with a red-hot skewer, but this is a slow process and needs special care.

The tapes are used doubled where the attachment goes, clear of the sail, but the ends of the tape are

splayed out over the sail. This spreads the loads and makes it easier to sew the 'tails' of the tapes to the sail.

Securing the luff after an accident

If the luff foil splits, breaks, wears badly at the bottom or fails in any way, it can be nearly impossible to set a headsail. Admittedly a sail might be set flying, with nothing to hold it except the halyard, tack fitting and sheets. However, this is a hazardous business, especially in windy weather. The sail can get under the keel, or even round the rudder or propeller.

If short lengths of sail tier are sewn to each side of the sail at the luff, they can be knotted round the luff foil. To be safe, there should be tiers stitched at the seams and in between the seams. It's better to have too many securing points rather than too few, in order to spread the loads.

A good type of sail tier material is that narrow, soft, double tape that is so easy to sew and to handle. The ½ in (12 mm) width suits yachts up to about 36 ft (11 m).

On well-equipped boats there are a few metres of this handy material stowed in the bosun's locker or sailmaker's bag for all sorts of emergencies.

This trick can be used in a variety of situations. If a sail that is normally hanked on is found to have lost, damaged or seized hanks,

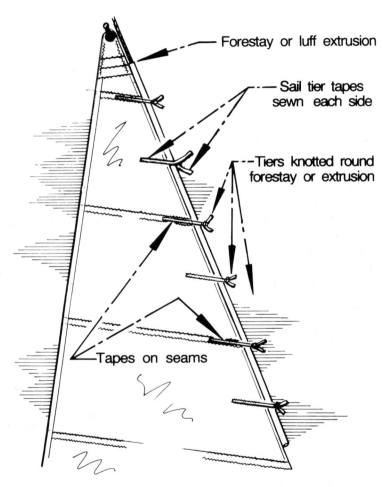

Forestay or luff extrusion

Sail tier tapes sewn each side

Tiers knotted round forestay or extrusion

Tapes on seams

tiers can be pressed into service. If the luff tape that goes into a luff foil is torn or damaged, the same arrangement will save the day.

Stitching through thick sails

Sails often get damaged at corners, where the sailcloth is multi-layered. It is no easy job to push an ordinary sail needle through so many closely-packed thicknesses, and it may be beyond the ability of anyone on board, even professionals. The chances are that if the job is being done offshore, half the available needles will be broken before the trouble has been fully appreciated.

There is a simple trick for dealing with thick sails. First, the location of each stitch is marked on the sail with a biro or pencil. Typically, the distances apart will be ¼ in (6 mm), as shown top left in the drawing. The stitches will probably be in a straight line, not zig-zagged.

A piece of wood at least ¾ in (20 mm) thick is laid on a strong base, and the sail put on top. With a sharp bradawl and a hammer, a row of holes is made at the marks. It is not necessary to bash the bradawl spike right through, though it should certainly go most of the way.

A nail can be used instead of a bradawl, but it is harder to get out after each hole is made. Instead of holding the nail in a hand, it is better to grasp it

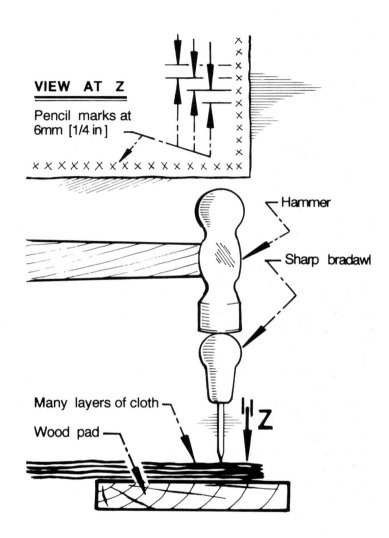

VIEW AT Z

Pencil marks at 6mm [1/4 in]

Hammer

Sharp bradawl

Many layers of cloth

Wood pad

Z

with a pair of pliers or Mole-grip. It may be difficult to find a bradawl with a truly sharp point. A grindstone or file is used to put an extra-long fine point on the end of the spike. However, this sharpened point should not be so thin and delicate that it cannot stand up to the hard work involved.

Spinnaker repair at sea

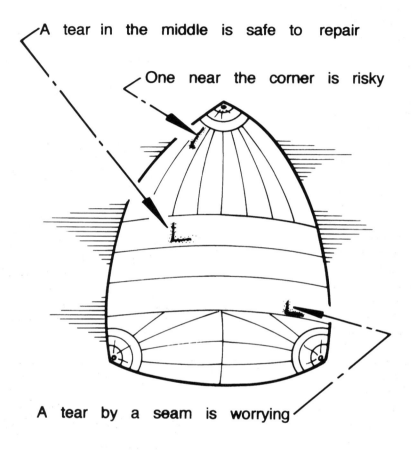

A tear in the middle is safe to repair

One near the corner is risky

A tear by a seam is worrying

When a spinnaker gets a small rip the crew naturally want to mend it right away, and be able to use the sail for the rest of the race or cruise. To this end, they normally set to with spinnaker repair tape to close up the rent. If the tear is in the middle, the cloth in this area will not be highly stressed unless the wind is strong.

As a general (but certainly not a universal) rule, few owners put up a spinny that has just a temporary tape-up in anything much over force 6. If there is an important race to win, a keen crew may put the sail up and hope the taping will hold. When there is an alternative, but perhaps less suitable, spinnaker available, most crews will use the other spinnaker and spend time making a sewn repair to the damaged sail..... provided, of course, they have the correct needles and thread!

This drawing may influence a decision as to whether a sail should be reset after an onboard repair. Rips near corners are much more likely to reopen and then spread, especially in gusty conditions.

Using spinnaker repair tape

Spinnaker repair tape is sold in rolls, typically 2–3 in (50–75 mm) wide. It is made of the same cloth as spinnakers, and on one side it is sticky with a 'peel-off' paper backing. It is an essential item in the repair kit of any racing yacht, and handy on board a cruiser for more than just sail repairs.

The sail should be dry before the tape is applied, so on yachts where there is the luxury of a source of hot air, the damaged area should be warmed till all local moisture has been driven off. An ideal tool is a hand-held hair-dryer; this is found on some large yachts..... perhaps brought on board without the skipper's knowledge!

Plenty of crews have taken the risk of drying a spinnaker over the galley cooker, and sometimes had a cheerful blaze as a result because nylon cloth is highly flammable. The usual technique is to rub the damaged area of the sail on both sides with dry towels.

The damaged part is laid on a flat surface, and the appropriate length of tape is cut off the roll. Ideally two or three pairs of hands hold the sail flat, while another pair holds the end of the tape. Yet another pair of

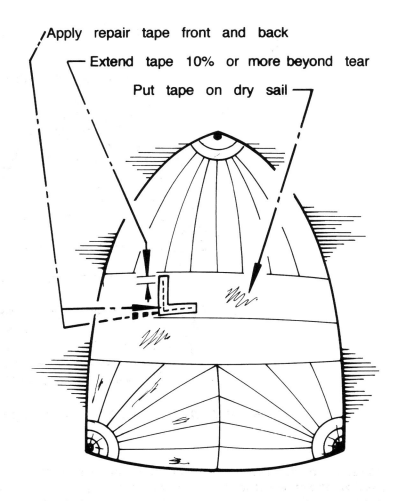

Apply repair tape front and back

Extend tape 10% or more beyond tear

Put tape on dry sail

hands peels the backing paper off the tape and starts applying the tape well clear of the end of the rip. An overlap of 10 per cent of the length of the tear is usually a minimum.

The tape is applied on the front and back of the

sail. Some people add extra tape strips at right angles to the main lengths, especially on large sails, and even more so if the wind is strong.

Repairing zig-zag stitching

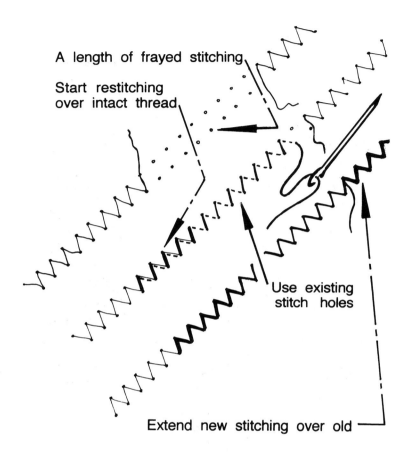

A length of frayed stitching

Start restitching
over intact thread

Use existing
stitch holes

Extend new stitching over old

A frayed length of zig-zag stitching caused by chafing is the most common trouble found in sails.

The top line of stitching in the drawing shows the problem: there are just two rows of needle holes left to show where the thread used to be.

In the second row of stitching, repairs have begun. The sailmaker has started stitching well back, where the stitching is intact. He brings the needle up through the cloth, takes it up and to the left, then down through the cloth. On the underside he moves it right and brings it up the next hole.

He only has to do two more stitches and he will meet the intact stitching at the top. The dotted lines show the new stitching on the underside. In the bottom row he has done a second row of stitching to complete the zig-zag repair by taking his needle up through a hole on the upper line and then across to the right on top of the cloth. He finishes by over-sewing the sound stitching at the top for a couple of inches (about 5 cm).

Emergency sailmaker's palm

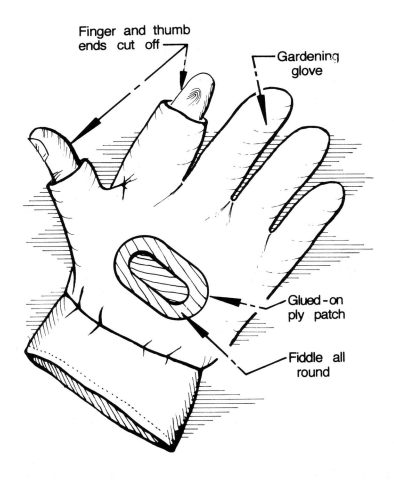

Finger and thumb
ends cut off

Gardening
glove

Glued-on
ply patch

Fiddle all
round

When forcing a needle through thick cloth, a sailmaker uses a palm, which is a leather strap that goes round the hand and holds a small steel disc. This disc (which is indented to prevent the needle slipping) is used to press down on the top of the needle with all the strength that the operator can muster.

It is hard to get a left-handed palm, so the drawing shows a home-made one that can easily be fabricated at sea in an emergency. Though it is unlikely that there will be gardening gloves on board, a sailing glove will do, or a crude glove can be made up from any cloth on board.

Instead of a special metal disc, a piece of ply or hardwood is glued or sewn in place. To prevent the needle slipping off the hard patch there is a rim, or tiny fiddle, all round. The end of the thumb and first finger of the glove are cut off to make it easy to grip the needle.

Large sail details

Handling a big sail in windy conditions can be hard, and sometimes impossible. Just getting a grip on the leech to haul it down is sometimes a fight because the cloth is so difficult to hold.

If tape handles are sewn on the leech the job is much easier, especially as the loops will hold tiers and lashings, put on to secure the sail until it can be bundled into a bag.

Each piece of tape should be 32 in (800 mm) long, with a 4 in (100 mm) length of stitching each end and in the middle. This gives two grab handles, each about 10 in (250 mm) long. This arrangement is big enough for two hands, so two people can work adjacent to one another, each with a loop large enough to be gripped by the fattest and widest hands. The enlarged detail on the left shows a pair of sail-handles.

Because the corners are so heavily stressed on a big sail, an ordinary hydraulically pressed eye, or an old-fashioned hand-worked one, may not be tough enough to stand up to six months' hard usage. One answer is to fit back-up eyes which are slightly smaller, and set further into the sail. They are joined to the big

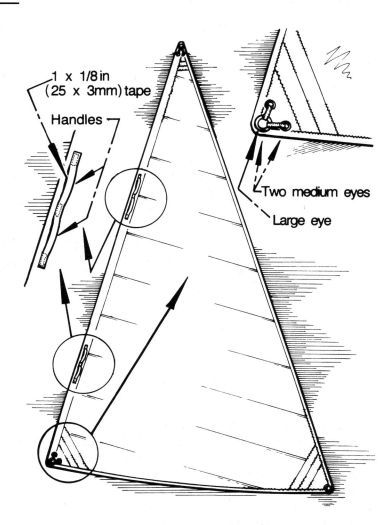

1 x 1/8 in (25 x 3mm) tape

Handles

Two medium eyes

Large eye

eye with strong tightly sewn tapes. This spreads the load of the sheets or halyard.

This trick is especially handy for a sailmaker who does not have facilities for making a big strong eye. Onboard repairs can sometimes be made using this technique too. The enlarged detail (top right), shows how it works.

These ideas are shown on a headsail, but they can be used on a mainsail or spinnaker – in fact, any large sail (and not so large) where they are appropriate.

Controlling sheet leads

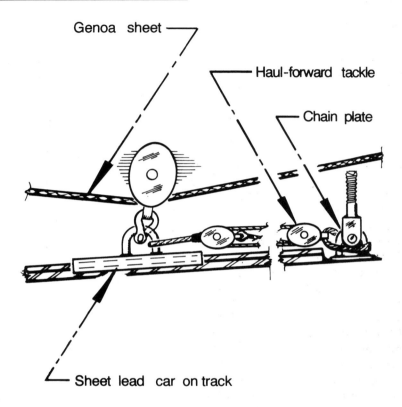

Genoa sheet

Haul-forward tackle

Chain plate

Sheet lead car on track

Genoa sheet lead cars have to be moved along their tracks as the wind changes in strength, and as the yacht changes course relative to the wind. On many yachts there are no facilities for shifting these cars, and when there is even a medium load on the sheet, the job can be hard without mechanical help.

It is usually easy to coax the car to slide aft, as the lead of the sheet applies a force in that direction. Getting the car forward needs a four-part tackle on a 33 ft (10 m) yacht, and for large yachts the same purchase may need taking to a winch.

The aft block of the tackle is secured to the fore end of the car, as shown in the drawing. The forward block may be held to a chain plate, perhaps by a shackle. On many yachts it will not be easy to get a shackle on to or round the chain plate, so a doubled length of strong tape may be used.

If a chain plate cannot be used it will probably be necessary to fix a U-bolt or some such through the deck. There will normally have to be underdeck re-inforcing, and the fitting must be capable of withstanding a strong pull aft.

Other things being equal, shifting the car forward tightens down the leech and slackens the foot; also, it makes the sail fuller. Moving the car aft opens the leech and tightens the foot; it also tends to flatten the sail.

Correct luff tension

To get the best speed out of a Terylene/Dacron sail, the luff must be the right tension. The stronger the wind, the tighter the luff should be. Once the correct halyard tension has been found, this rope should be marked alongside a line on the deck. This allows the correct tension to be found quickly on future occasions and with certainty, even by an inexperienced crew member.

Though the drawing shows a single line on the deck, with light and heavy weather marks on the halyard, some keen teams have just one mark on the halyard and a succession on deck, numbered to suit the Beaufort wind scale, or the wind speed as shown on the nearby instruments.

The marks are made with indelible pens, and sometimes with paint on the cabin-top deck. Coloured thread may be sewn through the halyard, though it is liable to get worn on the winch.

Varying the luff tension alters the shape of the sail. Extra tightness causes flattening and tends to bring the maximum curvature further forward, which suits stronger winds. However, this technique does not apply to Mylar and other sails that are made of so-called 'stretch-proof' fabrics. The same applies to sails that consist of non-stretch threads sandwiched between plastic outer skins. Even these sails often need some variations in luff tension to suit light (and very light) conditions. This tensioning applies to headsails and mainsails.

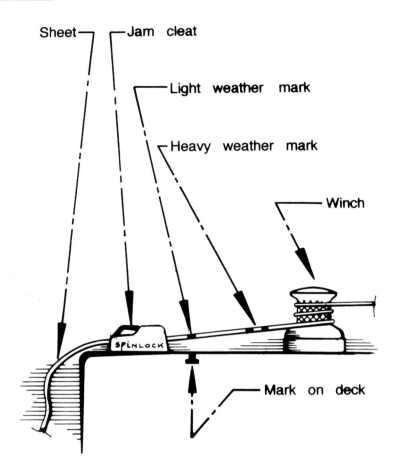

To avoid extending a genoa lead track

This is a simple trick for saving time, money and work when it has been discovered that the genoa sheet lead track needs extending forwards. Instead of fitting a new longer track, or moving the existing track further forward, the lead block is changed so that the sheet is held lower down. This has the same effect as lengthening the track by a small amount. Admittedly this idea does not work if the track has to be extended forward some distance.

There are several ways the lead of the sheet from forward can be lowered: for a start, a smaller block can be used. It is important to select one with ball bearings to reduce the friction, and the reduction must not be too large. In practice, one would seldom drop down more than one size.

Alternatively, a slider can be bought that has the block permanently attached, without a shackle between the block and slider. This has the effect of dropping the bottom of the sheave by the length of a shackle. One attraction of these changes is that they can normally be made on a trial basis by borrowing the necessary blocks or sliders to see if

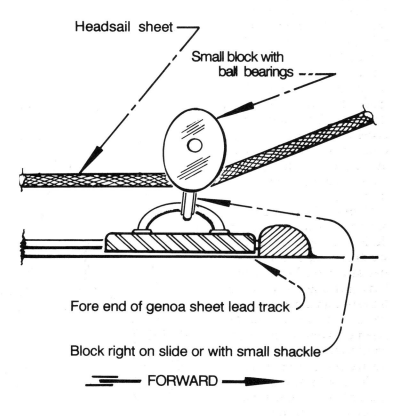

Headsail sheet

Small block with ball bearings

Fore end of genoa sheet lead track

Block right on slide or with small shackle

FORWARD ➤

they give enough height reduction.

If the sheets are worn, consideration should be given to using the next size down so that the reduction block size is acceptable and within the minimum recommended sheave size.

For the ideal and minimum sheave sizes relative to rope size, see *The Boat Data Book* by Ian Nicolson, published by Adlard Coles Nautical.

Judging distances aloft

A tear appears in the spinnaker, but it is not bad enough to haul the spinnaker down..... especially as there is a race to be won! The crew look aloft and agree that the tear is 12 in (30 cm) long, and is 3 ft (1 m) in from the edge of the sail.

They now know how long to cut the pieces of spinnaker repair tape *before* the sail is lowered, so when the sail is down the repair tape is already cut to length and is ready to apply without any delay. The work can be done swiftly, because the crew know exactly where to find the tear even though the sail is in a jumbled pile inside the boat.

How can anyone judge distances aloft, a long way above the cockpit? Obviously practice helps, but so does this super-simple trick: before the mast is set up at the beginning of the season, the lengths of the crosstrees are measured; so are the crosstree end pads. This gives a simple gauge, or comparative measure.

When it comes to sheeting in the headsail, the trimmer may know that the sail has to be 6 in (150 mm) off the end of the crosstree. This is, perhaps, three times the width of the end pad, or maybe one-fifth the length of the crosstree. This technique works in the dark provided there is a good flashlight with an intense narrow beam available. It also works in bad weather and in the rain. It's a handy skill and an easy one to apply.

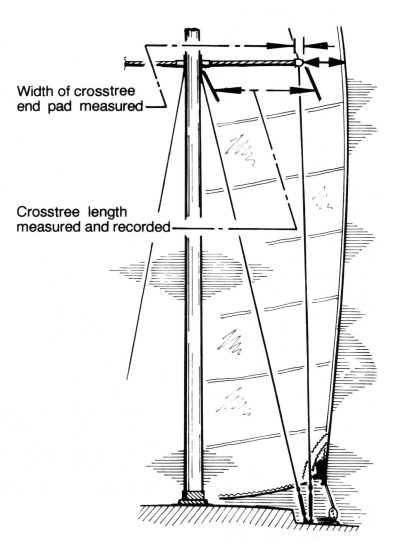

Width of crosstree end pad measured—

Crosstree length measured and recorded—

A scale on photographs

When taking photos of a yacht to find the mast bend (see page 4), the forestay sag, or just to look at the set of the sails, it is essential to have an accurate scale on the picture, which must be taken from dead abeam.

A simple way to arrange a scale is to have marks along the boom. These can be painted or put on with a coloured marker, but the most usual technique is to apply self-adhesive tape. It must have a strong contrasting colour, and to be sure it shows up it will need to be 2 in (50 mm) wide, with known precise intervals at least as big. The longer the 'scale' the better, and 5 per cent of the yacht's length is the minimum.

However, booms are not always trimmed along the centreline of the yacht, nor level, so marks on the boom are not always ideal. An alternative location is on the topsides, which must be clean and dry before sticking on the tape.

The marks must be amidships where the topsides are not curved in towards the bow or stern, so that the 'plane' of the scale is accurately at right angles to the line of sight of the camera. Tumble-home or flare does not matter in this context

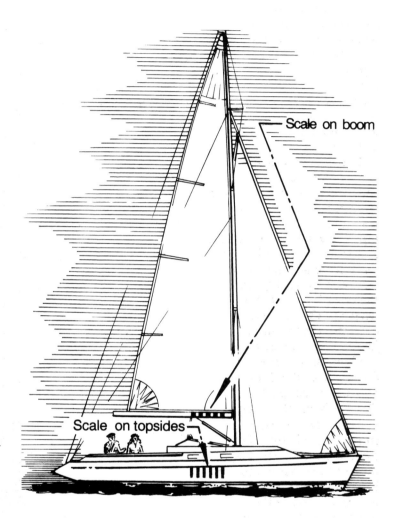

Scale on boom

Scale on topsides

provided the stripes are vertical.

Sometimes the photographer wants to take a shot from forward or aft. For this, the marks on the boom or topsides are not

accurate, and the alternative is to have a board with vertical marks at suitable intervals. One of the crew must hold this board up, directly facing the camera.

Batten stiffness test rig

In light winds a racing yacht needs 'soft' battens that bend easily. The stronger the wind, the stiffer the battens have to be. The drawing shows an ultra-simple tester to measure batten stiffness. It depends on using the same equipment and the same dimensions all the time, so that the stiffness of one batten can be tested against others. It is essential to keep a careful note of each batten tested, and the deflection it gives.

The rig is set up at the edge of a table..... always the same table, with the same sharp edge. A stiff straight piece of wood is fixed so that it extends out from the table. The extension of this perfectly straight wood bar beyond the table must always be the same. The batten under test is secured with an ordinary clamp close to, but not touching, the wood bar. A weight, always the same weight, is hung on the end of the batten under test, precisely ½ in (12 mm) from the end of the batten by a length of thin string.

To stop the string sliding off the batten it is held on with a piece of Sellotape. The amount of deflection or bend is measured from the underside of the wood bar

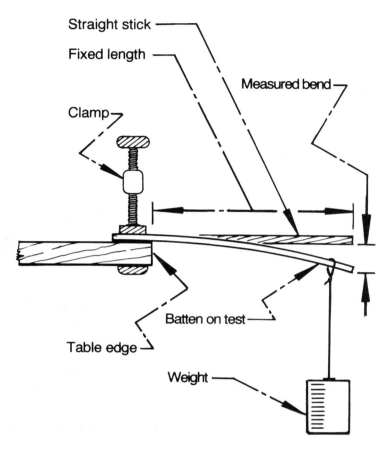

to the underside of the batten, once the weight has stopped swinging about.

If a batten is too stiff it can be thinned down. If it is too flexible it can be stiffened by adding more material, but it is normally best to get a thicker and stiffer batten.

Unmeasured sail area

Some people call it the 'vang', others call it the 'kicking strap', but all agree it is essential for safe and competitive sailing, because the boom aft end must be prevented from lifting sky-wards.

If the triangle between the vang/kicking strap, the boom and the mast is filled by a piece of cloth, all sorts of benefits result. When reaching or going to wind-ward the mainsail luff length is slightly increased. Also, the high pressure air on the windward side of the mainsail is prevented from leaking under the fore end of the boom, to the leeward low pressure side. This gives a little extra drive, just as the extra sail area helps when going downwind.

Terylene or Dacron or any other sailmaker's cloth can be used for this fill-in. It has the added advantage that it stops ropes getting tangled, and a pocket can be sewn on the side for the deck knife, as well as a flashlight when night sailing.

Ideally the triangular cloth has a 'luff rope' in the mainsail track at the fore end, and a similar arrange-ment along the top under the boom. However, slides may have to be used – or even a lashing round the mast. The aft part will lengthen the life of the rope part of the vang by keeping off the ultra-violet rays. One disadvantage is that the view from the cockpit may be reduced.

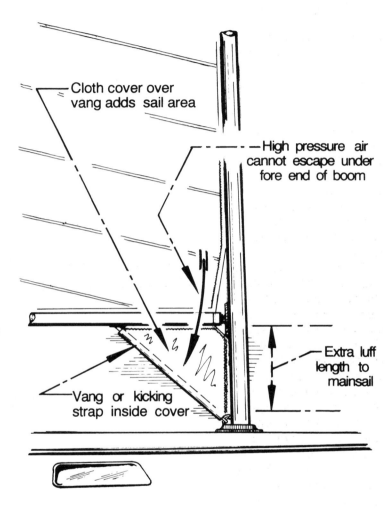

Cloth cover over vang adds sail area

High pressure air cannot escape under fore end of boom

Extra luff length to mainsail

Vang or kicking strap inside cover

Fender cloths

Yachts that lie in marinas need a full row of fenders over the side. There must be no large gaps between them, in case one fender rope chafes through and leaves the yacht undefended.

Unfortunately fenders gather dirt, usually in the form of dust. This acts like a grinding paste on the topsides, slowly chafing off the glossy surface. The way to protect the hull is to hang 'fender cloths' over the side, inboard of the fenders. These are made of any soft, strong, washable cloth.

Two sets of cloths are needed, one in use and the other being laundered to get rid of accumulated dirt, and ensure the cloths stay soft. There must be no metal eyes at the top corners of the cloths as they might scratch the topsides, or damage the inside of the washing machine. Instead, the lashings, which are typically of ½ in (12 mm) Terylene tape, are stitched on to the fender cloths. This can be done by hand or using a zig-zag sailmaker's sewing machine.

The cloths are hung well down, but clear of low waves, with their lashing spread out fore-and-aft. They must extend beyond the fenders because occasionally these will swing fore-and-aft in severe conditions. To ensure ample area, some sailmakers use the full available width of cloth. The edges need seaming to deal with chafe and to ensure a long life.

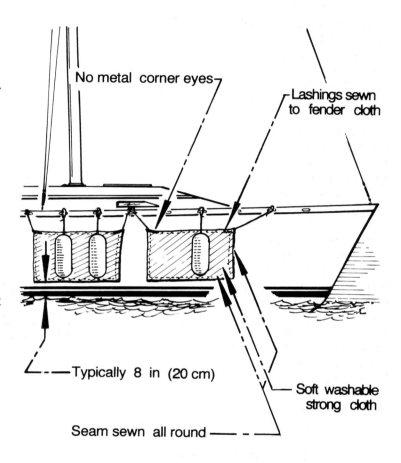

No metal corner eyes

Lashings sewn to fender cloth

Typically 8 in (20 cm)

Seam sewn all round

Soft washable strong cloth

The higher, the faster

The wind flows faster at 100 ft (30 m) above sea level than it does low down, and this graph shows just how the speed varies according to the height above water level. The gain in speed is about 10 per cent between halfway up a Maxi's mast and the top. Big gains, roughly from 50 per cent of the high-up speed to 90 per cent of this speed, occur from approximately 5 ft (1.5 m) to 50 ft (15 m) above sea level.

All sorts of deductions can be made from this graph. It partly explains why big yachts with high masts sail away from small craft in light and moderate winds. Because sails high up are more effective than those even a short distance lower down, masthead rigs have a certain advantage over three-quarter rigs of the same total height. Spinnakers set at, say, 40 ft (12 m) will do better than those set 35 ft (11 m) above sea level.

Following on from this, if the foot of a sail does not look well set but the head is superb, the effect is better than when the head looks lousy but the foot looks lovely. This graph also explains why a mainsail twisted off at the top makes sense, since the higher wind

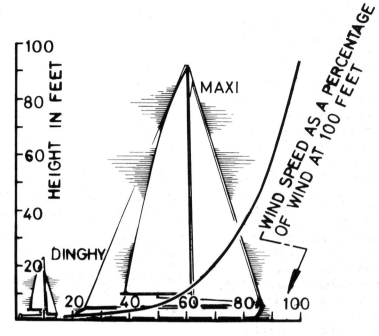

is exerting more pressure, and one wants to get less heeling moment but more forward thrust from it.

Other lessons from this graph include:

- In strong winds it is more effective to lower the total height of the sail plan rather than reduce the area.
- Putting a big roach high up on a mainsail, even if this means having longer battens, increases the

drive by more than the proportional sail area increase.
- Mast tapering makes double sense because where the wind speed is higher, the resistance is greater..... and so on.

The three-reef dress

'What shall I wear.....' thinks every woman when she and her partner are invited to a party, or club event. It is a fact that while every woman wants to be dressed *differently* from all the others she meets, yet she wants her dress to be the same *length*.

Pondering this problem, it occurred to me that a dress which could be easily and quickly varied in length would be the biggest boon. Mainsails have to be changed to suit differing wind strengths, and, connecting sails with dresses, it was obvious that what every woman wants is a reefable dress.

The following situation will then arise frequently: a couple drive to a party or prize-giving or launching or whatever is being celebrated. They park discreetly where they can watch guests arrive. It is clear that this month (since fashions now change that frequently) the calf length is 'in'. A single reef is tucked in the dress, and the lady emerges from the car right in the current fashion.

There are other practical applications for this all-purpose dress. For instance no woman wants to go ashore in a dinghy with water washing over the floor-boards if she is wearing a long dress. So even if she is going to wear a full-length dress for a ball, she can tuck in three reefs for the voyage ashore.

Three reefs for going ashore through surf and wild parties

Two reefs for going ashore in a wet dinghy followed by a long walk to the clubhouse

One reef for sultry evenings in the cockpit or Scottish dancing in the clubhouse

No reef for formal club evening dress